LAW

THE ART OF JUSTICE

LAW

THE ART OF JUSTICE

MORRIS L. COHEN

HUGH LAUTER LEVIN ASSOCIATES, INC.

Distributed by Macmillan Publishing Company,
New York

This collection is dedicated to two individuals
who, in different ways,
have opened our eyes to images of justice:

the late Professor Robert Cover of the Yale Law School,
scholar of legal iconography,
and
Mrs. Bernice Loss, Curator of the Art Collection, Harvard Law School.

Copyright © 1992,
Hugh Lauter Levin Associates, Inc.

Design by Kathleen Herlihy-Paoli

Typeset by
U.S. Lithograph, typographers, New York City

Printed in Hong Kong

ISBN 0-88363-091-5

Jacket illustration: Raphael. *Justice*. ca. 1510.
Fresco. The Vatican, Rome.

CONTENTS

LAW

THE ART OF JUSTICE

Throughout the ages, artists and writers have depicted the people, events, and institutions of their times. They chose topics that were at once familiar and mysterious; that could teach lessons and stir emotions; that could reveal and touch the individual's experience and yet transcend the specific time and place. Part of the power of art lies in highlighting the universal qualities to be found in a particular subject.

Although the origins of law and the concept of justice are still largely clouded in mystery, images of law and justice have been found in the literature and art of most ancient cultures. From those early societies, we learn of the rules by which their people lived, and of the ways in which those rules were enforced and disputes were resolved. We also find in the art of many cultures, portrayals of lawmakers and lawgivers, judges, lawyers, and officers. We see scenes of the law in operation, of the people who used it, those who were its beneficiaries and its victims.

This volume brings together a sampling of representations of law and justice—images that offer powerful insights into the role of law in particular periods and places of human history.

The pervasiveness and inescapability of the law have made it a natural theme for artists. The drama of the law in action, particularly in court trials, gave it power to excite the viewer. Pictorial images of justice, either by symbolic representations or by the portrayal of specific events in the struggle for justice, have always been popular subjects.

The history of law is multifaceted. Viewed metaphorically, that history is more like a library than a single book, with separate sections on the law of different cultures, countries, or systems. In ancient times, for example, there were the legal systems of Egypt, Babylon, China, Israel, Greece, and Rome; in later periods, canon law, Islamic law, common law, and civil law; and in modern times, the law or legal events of individual nations and of the conflict between nations. Within the sections of that "historical library," individual volumes might deal, singly or in com-

bination, with specific periods of time, legal subjects, and nations or systems.

Yet there are still other dimensions by which law can be viewed. Its history can be studied through the officials or individuals by which or on which the law operated: lawgivers like Moses; lawmakers like Justinian; judges like Solomon; lawyers like Cicero; victims like Joan of Arc; and average citizens carrying out the legal activities and obligations of their time, place, and station —buying a cow, selling a crop, writing a will, bearing witness, swearing an oath, or paying a tax. Many of these aspects of the law, from the most general to the quite specific, have been the subject of the artist's brush or the sculptor's hammer and chisel. Artists approached and treated their subjects in different ways and for varied purposes—to glorify, illuminate, criticize, mock, or simply to describe graphically some aspect of the law.

This book offers a collection of representative portrayals of symbols, people, texts, and events in the history of law. The works depict discrete images in the flow of events that constitute the struggle for justice under law. The nature of justice, however, changes over time. What was considered just at one time may later seem unjust. To enslave captives taken in battle once may have seemed a great advance over the earlier practice of simply killing the vanquished enemy; today, it seems barbaric. The methods of the law's operation also changed, as we can see for example in the progress from trial by an omnipotent judge to trial by battle or trial by wager, and later to trial by a jury of one's peers. These works of art, therefore, naturally reflect the changing concepts of justice held by different cultures and the varied procedures of law employed in different periods.

A brief narrative is provided for each work of art to describe the legal theme, person, or issue it illustrates. These discussions also present the social context of the scene portrayed. We have offered a wide range (both culturally and chronologically) of subjects, in the hope of conveying the broad sweep of the history of law. The variety of the subjects and the differences in graphic techniques employed also suggest the many ways in which artists saw and represented the law and justice of the world around them. Although not a systematic history, this survey begins in ancient times and proceeds more or less chronologically through many of the world's great legal systems. The first ten illustrations focus on individuals, each of whom was an important figure in the law of that time. Most of them were or became mythic figures in their particular cultures or in history generally.

Maat, the Egyptian goddess of justice, is a frequent and magisterial figure in papyrus paintings and in murals found in the tombs and temples of ancient Egypt. She symbolized a whole range of civic virtues, including not only justice, but truth, order, and righteousness as well. Moses, shown here both receiving and then transmitting the law, was and remains for many a more vivid representation of how law comes to society. In *The Judgment of Solomon*, powerfully conveyed in Rubens' lush canvas, we see the wise peacemaker resolving the conflict and ambiguity which often attend the application of law to specific cases. The abstract quality of Maat is very different from both the awesome theophany of Moses receiving the tablets of the law on Sinai and the chilling psychology of Solomon's judicial solution.

Socrates, who was both teacher and martyr, presents an example of the philosopher in the history of law. While teaching notions of justice and wisdom in the moral order, Socrates incurred the enmity of new rulers of Athens, was tried, and found guilty of denying the officially recognized gods and of corrupting the young. He is shown here, after refusing exile and a chance to escape, assuming an almost voluntary martyrdom.

Following the moving tableau of Socrates' death is the first of several unusual scenes of ancient trials or judgments, each of which conveys the dramatic tension inherent in the administration of criminal justice. First is the painting by Gerard David showing the arrest of Sisamnes, a corrupt judge of Persia, and his judgment by King Cambyses II. Then, after portrayals of Justinian and Confucius, is the trial of Phryne, a Greek priestess, in which she is defended by her lover, Hyperides, against a charge of profaning religious mysteries. Next, Cicero denounces Catiline before the Roman Senate for plotting a conspiracy of insurrection against the Republic.

Artists have also created striking images of lawgivers and scholars who have perfected or taught the law. In addition to Moses receiving the law on Sinai, these include a mosaic of Justinian, the great Christian emperor of Byzantium, who commissioned the *Corpus Juris Civilis*; a painting of Confucius, prime minister and sometime judge, who became a philosopher and itinerant teacher of law and ethics; a portrayal by Raphael (Raffaello Sanzio) of Pope Gregory IX receiving the Decretals, a major code of canon law. Later in the book, we see a romantic allegory, *The Napoleonic Code Crowned by Time*, which shows Napoleon floating on a cloud holding a tablet of law like Moses. Two very different representations of the law being taught are the fifteenth-century marble frieze of the *Law Lecturer* and *A Class at the University of Pennsylvania Law School* shown in a nineteenth-century oil painting.

The actual texts of the law have at times been so beautifully decorated and illustrated as to become themselves works of art. Examples of this are seen in the manuscript of the *Mirror of Saxony*, a North German compilation of medieval customary law; an illustrated manuscript of Henry de Bracton's great treatise, *On the Laws and Customs of England*; the *Coutumes de Normandie*, the influential fifteenth-century collection of French regional law; and the *Huejotzingo Codex*, used by Hernando Cortes during his conquest of Mexico.

The law has often been misused or perverted to serve the personal, national, or religious interests of the powerful. Unjust discrimination by religion, race, class, and gender was common. Very different examples of women who suffered under the law are shown here in a fifteenth-century Spanish manuscript, called *Conjugal Law* which depicts an adulterous wife in court; the painting of Joan of Arc by Ingres; Shakespeare's version of King Henry VIII's annulment of his marriage of Katharine of Aragon; and Hogarth's satirical tale of *Marriage à la Mode: The Marriage Contract*.

Symbolic images of justice have been depicted in all ages. Two representations of *Justicia*, the female figure of justice, appear in very different paintings by Lorenzetti and Raphael.

Examples of the law being used to persecute unpopular or unorthodox opinions or individuals are seen in the portrait of *Thomas More*, chancellor of England, who was martyred by King Henry VIII; the portrayal of *Galileo Before the In-*

quisition; the *Trial of George Jacobs*, one of the victims in the seventeenth-century witchcraft trials of Salem, Massachusetts; and *The Passion of Sacco and Vanzetti*, Ben Shahn's powerful image of the bodies of the two Italian anarchists after their execution.

Judicial councils, legislative assemblies, and political conventions have been frequent subjects of large paintings for public display, often commissioned for the glorification of the nation or its leaders. Examples of such patriotic art include: *The Magistrates of Paris*; *The Hague Magistrates Receiving the Officers of the Civic Guard*; *Louis XIV Presiding at the Council of Parties*; *The Seat of Justice in the Parliament of Paris*; *Tennis Court Oath*; and *Washington Addressing the Constitutional Convention*.

Evidences of the struggle against American slavery and its residual effects in racial segregation are seen in the *Trial of the Captive Slaves*; *John Brown Going to His Hanging*; and *The Problem We All Live With*, Norman Rockwell's portrayal of school desegregation.

The administration of criminal justice and the punishment it imposes are shown in a diverse selection of images including the fifteenth-century *A Wager of Battel*; Rowlandson's caricature of *Marshalsea Prison*; *Justice's Court in the Backwoods*; *Preliminary Trial of a Horse Thief*; and *Red Disaster*, Andy Warhol's eerie rendition of the electric chair.

Artists have recognized the varied roles of lawyers and have treated them with appropriate diversity. Those represented here include two seventeenth-century genre paintings, *The Lawyer's Office* and *The Village Lawyer*; the patriotic advocate in *Patrick Henry Arguing the* Parson's Cause; Rowlandson and Daumier's satirical portraits in, respectively, *Reading the Will* and *Three Lawyers*; Ward's group caricature of English lawyers and judges, *Bench and Bar*; and finally Thomas Hart Benton's *Trial by Jury*.

The visual portrayal of law in art provides concrete evidence of how the law functioned and how it was viewed in other times and places. Such representations aid historians, social scientists, and creative writers to better understand the law and its workings. Graphic images can go beyond documentation; they can convey the atmosphere and emotion of events through composition, color, and movement. The perception and understanding of all viewers (not only specialists) is thereby enhanced, since great art conveys universal values. In the society for which the art was produced, it could educate and engender any of a variety of responses—fear, respect, admiration, anger, laughter, loyalty, or opposition. Art was and is a powerful form of commentary.

We hope that the examples in this book of the interaction of art and law will provide a new context for appreciating both disciplines. This panorama of legal personalities, events, and institutions can also broaden and deepen our view of the history of law and the struggle for justice. Beyond that, the iconography of the law can bring us closer to understanding the classic trinity of truth, beauty, and justice. ▪

LAW

THE ART OF JUSTICE

ca. 1306–1290 B.C.

Maat, the Egyptian goddess of justice, was female, as were most symbols of justice in later European culture. However, she represented a broader range of civic virtues than her successors. Maat symbolized not only justice, but also truth, order, and righteousness. She was thus a more central and ubiquitous figure in Egyptian society than was Justitia, for example, in the Roman world. Maat signified the emergence of order out of chaos.

Maat, the daughter of the sun god, Re, and the wife of the god of wisdom, Thoth, symbolized one of the oldest abstract terms in human speech. Originally, the word *mat* or *maat* meant right or correct. Gradually, its meaning expanded to include truth, order, and justice. Kings and pharaohs were expected to exhibit maat and were themselves often considered to be personifications of maat. By dispensing maat to the people, rulers became godlike. The quality of maat was, therefore, evidence of good leadership and of government that was both orderly and just.

The ostrich feather of justice which rises from Maat's headdress was her emblem and was used symbolically in several different ways. The chief justice of Egypt wore an image of Maat on his collar and began court sessions by donning Maat's feather. Judgment was signified in each proceeding by handing the feather to the successful party as a symbol of a favorable decision.

Egyptian representations of *divine* justice illustrate the day of judgment on which the souls of the deceased are judged. The heart of the deceased individual is often shown being weighed on scales against Maat's feather of justice, to determine whether the life was true and just, or evil.

This representation of Maat is from the tomb of Seti I, ruler of Egypt in the nineteenth Dynasty, ca. 1306–1290 B.C. Seti was a successful military leader who conquered Palestine and Lebanon. He was also a noted builder, who continued his father's constructions at Karnak, built a great temple at Abydos, and made a magnificent galleried tomb for himself in the Valley of the Kings, at Thebes. Seti's reign is generally considered to have been one of expansion, economic development, and enrichment. The portrayal of Maat was a common theme in royal tombs and signified that the king had ruled with justice, order, and righteousness.

Colorplate 1. Upper fragment of a bas-relief from the tomb of Seti I, nineteenth Dynasty. White limestone. 29⅛ × 18½" (74 × 47 cm). Archaeological Museum, Florence. Scala/Art Resource, NY.

MOSES RECEIVES THE TABLES OF THE LAW; MOSES PRESENTS THEM TO THE PEOPLE

Mid–ninth century

From ancient to modern times—from Maat and Moses to Madison and Marshall—lawgivers have been popular subjects for artists and sculptors. Moses receiving the law from God on Mount Sinai and proclaiming it to the people are perhaps the most famous and persistent of these portrayals. Although graven images were forbidden by the first of the Ten Commandments (Exod. 20:4), almost every age and culture which has been touched by the biblical account has reproduced the lawgiving on Sinai in its art.

There are several subjects in the graphic representation of the revelation on Sinai—Moses, the tablets of the law, and the people of Israel. Also central to the scene are two other, more elusive elements: God, who is only rarely represented visually, and the covenant which appears, if at all, only in the responses of the Israelites. In addition to these subjects, the event itself has many facets which provide different levels of meaning to its varied audiences and interpreters.

For example, one could focus on the theological dimension portrayed in the theophany, the awesome drama of God's appearance to man; or on the psychological aspect of the relationships between God and Moses, between Moses and his people, and between God and Israel. Historical and political implications can be seen in the covenant by which Israel accepts the law delivered by Moses from God, and by which the Israelites become a distinct people with a new historical role. In the context of this book, however, it is the giving of the law and the role of the lawgiver that are our focus. Although there were older law codes (for example the Babylonian code attributed to Hammurabi), the Mosaic code introduced new concepts of human rights, justice, and fair treatment, as well as a more advanced monotheistic religion.

There are varying views of the content and extent of the body of law given on Sinai. Some see it merely as the transmission of the Ten Commandments, engraved on two tablets. The more common view includes the whole of the covenant code in chapters 21–24 of Exodus. Broader conceptions encompass the whole of the Torah, the first five books of the Hebrew Bible, also called the Pentateuch. Many in the Orthodox Jewish community consider that the oral law, including the Mishnah and the Talmud, were also transmitted on Sinai. However we define the content of that law, the event is a seminal image in the histories of religion, law, and art.

The basic code of the covenant is a mixture of moral commandments, civil and criminal law, and directions for religious observance. Its force lies in the fact that it is expressly sanctioned by God, with specific penalties enumerated for some violations.

Although Rembrandt's painting, *Moses with the Tables of the Law* (1659), and Michelangelo's marble statue of Moses in Rome at S. Pietro in Vincoli (ca. 1513–1516) are more frequently seen images, we show here an older representation from the ninth-century illuminated manuscript of the Montier-Grandval Bible, held at the British Library in London. The manuscript, from the School of Tours in France, is generally dated between A.D. 834 and A.D. 843. In the upper panel, Moses receives the law in the form of a scroll from the hand of God. As in the biblical text, smoke and fire appear on the mountain. The younger man to the side is Joshua. In the lower panel, the scene moves to an open hall with classical features where Moses is reading the law to the people. Joshua stands behind him and the bearded man facing Moses seems to be Aaron. The more primitive quality of this depiction may better convey to us the antiquity and mystery of the revelation on Sinai than do the more familiar, robust Renaissance representations of Moses.

Colorplate 2. From the Bible of Montier-Grandval. Miniature on parchment. 16 × 11½" (40.6 × 29.2 cm). British Library, London.

1615–1617

Peter Paul Rubens

Perhaps the most dramatic of the many legal disputes in the Bible is Solomon's judgment on the conflicting claims of two harlots, each of whom alleges that she is the mother of an infant in dispute between them. The story has suspense, color, and emotional charge. Similar controversies, such as the recent Baby M case and others arising from the new reproductive technologies, give this ancient conundrum a peculiarly modern relevance. The biblical account in the First Book of Kings, 3:16–28, relates the testimonies of two women living in the same house, each having recently been delivered of a child, and one of the infants having died. Each woman claims that the living child is hers and that the dead child belongs to the other woman. With no other evidence before him and no further investigation possible, Solomon proceeds to his unusual judgment.

"Fetch me a sword," the King orders and then commands that the child be cut in half and divided between the women. One woman cries out, "Oh, my Lord, give her the living child, and in no wise slay it," and the other says, "It shall be neither mine nor thine; divide it." Their very different responses tell the king which is the true mother, and he decides in favor of the first woman. The chapter ends as follows: "And all Israel heard of the judgment which the king had judged; and they feared the king; for they saw that the wisdom of God was in him, to do justice."

Solomon, the son of David and Bathsheba, succeeded to the Judean throne in 960 B.C. The builder of the first Temple in Jerusalem, Solomon is known primarily as a man of wisdom and as a peacemaker. The proverbial "wisdom" of Solomon derives largely from stories such as this one, but the judgment is that of a clever autocrat practicing practical psychology, rather than of a learned jurist.

The account of the judgment raises troublesome questions. Would Solomon have divided and killed the infant if the woman had not responded as she did? What is the relation between this scene of a royal potentate dispensing personal justice without apparent control or formal law and the more developed legal rules and structures described earlier in the Hebrew Bible? Although the legend, with its direct and simple means of reaching a just result in a seemingly insoluble dispute, enhances Solomon's popular reputation as a wise judge, his method clearly violates the procedures of even ancient Jewish law. Rabbi Judah the Prince, who compiled the Mishnah, the great law code of the second century, said, "If I had been present when he said, 'Fetch me a sword,' I would have put a rope around his neck, for if God had not been merciful and prompted the mother to give up her child rather than see it die, it would surely have been killed by him."

This Baroque painting of the judgment scene is by Peter Paul Rubens (1577–1640), perhaps the greatest of the Flemish masters. Rubens was a cosmopolitan man who mastered the classics, knew six languages, and was a skilled diplomat. In view of the subject of this painting, it is interesting to note that the artist's father, Jan Rubens, was a lawyer and financial advisor (and perhaps lover) to Princess Anne, wife of William I, prince of Orange. For his involvement in court intrigues and scandals, Jan Rubens was imprisoned. Peter Paul Rubens was himself experienced in court life, having served as court painter to the duke of Mantua and to the Spanish regent in Antwerp, and probably knew, first hand, the royal justice of his time.

Colorplate 3. Oil on canvas. 91¾ × 118⅞″ (233 × 302 cm). Royal Museum of Fine Arts, Copenhagen.

1787

Jacques-Louis David

The trial and death of the great Greek teacher and philosopher, Socrates, by the city of Athens in 399 B.C. is one of the great political prosecutions of all time. By accepting the prescribed punishment of a self-administered poison rather than escaping from the city or using other equally available means of avoiding the death penalty, Socrates chose martyrdom—a role in which he has become a historic symbol of resistance to oppression and tyranny. It is ironic that this brilliant and eccentric conservative, who publicly derided democracy and the democratic party of his time, should have become a hero of free speech, thought, and teaching.

Although Athens in the fifth century B.C. enjoyed what we now call the Greek Enlightenment, the thirty-year period following 432 was a time of repressive legislation against science and free thought. Persecutions and trials for heresy were common, and the defendants included other leading thinkers of Athens—Diagoras, Protagoras, and Anaxagoras.

Socrates had long opposed and annoyed the ruling factions of Athens, and openly held democracy in contempt. In an indictment brought against him by Meletus, a poet; Anytus, a tanner; and Lycon, an orator, Socrates was accused of denying those gods recognized by the state and introducing new ones, and of corrupting the young people of Athens. Rather than conciliate his accusers and judges, Socrates defied them throughout the proceedings, and thereby made the verdict of guilty and the death penalty inevitable.

Instead of counter-proposing a lesser punishment (which would probably have been accepted) Socrates boldly and defiantly argued that, for his services to Athens, he deserved reward and not punishment and should be declared a public benefactor (which carried with it support by the state). The annoyed judges voted the death penalty by a majority larger than that for his conviction. After imprisonment for thirty days, during which he was visited by friends and students, he drank a cup of hemlock, and died.

The best known ancient accounts of the trial and death of Socrates is in Plato's *Phaedo*, but they are also related in Xenophon's *Memorabilia* and in the *Life of Socrates* by Diogenes Laertius. The story has been told many times through the ages in drama, prose, and poetry. It has also been

illustrated by many artists. *The Death of Socrates*, by Jacques-Louis David (1748–1825) is probably the most popular and distinguished rendition of that scene. It is also considered to be among the best work of this great artist of the French Revolution. David painted many classical and historical events, particularly subjects with libertarian or revolutionary themes. A popular hero who involved himself actively in the events of his day, David was close to the leadership of the Revolution and painted many of its important figures.

The Death of Socrates, completed in 1787 and exhibited to public acclaim, reflects David's use of art to make political statements. He could identify with Socrates and undoubtedly saw in his martyrdom against oppression a lesson for contemporary France.

Colorplate 4. Oil on canvas. 57×77½″ (129.5×196.2 cm). The Metropolitan Museum of Art, New York. Wolfe Fund, 1931. Catherine Lorillard Wolfe Collection.

1498

Gerard David

This striking scene of ancient justice by the Flemish painter Gerard David (ca. 1460–1523) was one of two panels commissioned to hang in the Hall of Justice in Bruges, David's home city. The painting the *Arrest (or Seizure) of Sisamnes*, together with its mate, the *Punishment (or Flailing) of Sisamnes*, form a unit called the *Judgment of Cambyses*, and were completed in 1498. They illustrate the story of Sisamnes, a corrupt judge of the Persian king, Cambyses, who ruled from 529 to 522 B.C. The event is described by Herodotus, the Greek historian of the fifth century B.C., and has been the subject of other paintings and drawings. The thrust of the story differs in its varied tellings.

Cambyses, a king of the Medes and Persians in the sixth century B.C., punished his judge, Sisamnes, for allegedly selling a verdict. He ordered the corrupt judge to be flayed and his skin cut into strips which were stretched to form the seat of the throne of judgment. Cambyses then appointed Otanes, the son of Sisamnes, as the new judge to sit on that seat. The gruesome punishment is graphically portrayed in the second panel, not shown here. The taking of the bribe is represented in a small vignette in the background of the first panel, and the appointment of the son to the judgeship is similarly shown in the background of the second panel.

Herodotus accuses Cambyses of many atrocities, including fratricide, and attributes his cruelty and often irrational punishments to madness. Later accounts interpret the tale as the necessary and justifiable act of a ruler curbing a corrupt judge. A sixteenth-century German medal illustrating the legend finds that "Cambyses maintained the law and administered it justly, as one can perceive here from the punishment."[1] The latter view was probably more in keeping with David's motive in using this story to decorate the courtroom in Bruges. It was likewise undoubtedly the view of the authorities who commissioned the paintings, intending to impress on local judges the importance of honesty and conscientiousness in their judging. The figure of Sisamnes in the painting has been said to bear a likeness to Peter Lanchals, a conspirator who betrayed the interests of the city of Bruges to Maximilian I of Austria.

The Flemish concern with law, and punishment for its violation, was reflected frequently in their art. Convicted prisoners in some cities were ordered to pay the cost of bronze sculptures to give public notice of their crimes.

Gerard David was the last great painter of the Netherlandish School of Bruges, and was particularly famous for the two panels. There is disagreement among scholars over the source of David's eclectic and often archaic style. Some hold that he followed older masters in order to revitalize the declining art of Bruges. For others, he was an innovator carrying the best qualities of the founders of his school to new levels of creativity.

1. "The Cambyses Justice Medal," *Art Bulletin* 19 (1947):121.

Colorplate 5. Oil on panel. 71¾ × 62¾" (182 × 159.4 cm). Groeningemuseum, Bruges.

ca. A.D. 547

Flavius Patrus Sabbatius Justinianus (A.D. 483–565), better known as Justinian, was emperor of the Byzantine or eastern Roman Empire. In addition to his considerable success in restoring and reunifying the old Roman Empire in the West, he is best known today for his enormous contributions to legal development. Shortly after his accession to power in A.D. 527, Justinian appointed commissioners to collect the constitutions, edicts, and writings of the Roman lawyers and judges. This mass of material had to be revised to meet the needs of Justinian's Christian society. Justinian saw himself as God's vicar on earth and realized that law and religion were essential to the cohesion of a society. He knew that, in addition to military strength, an effective body of law was needed to assure the power and control of the new Roman Empire.

Four great legal works were compiled at his direction—the *Code* or *Codex* (promulgated in 529 and revised in 534); the *Digest* or *Pandects* (completed in 533); the *Institutes* (533); and the *Novellae* or *Novels* (534), a collection of supplementary laws. The work was largely supervised by Tribonian (A.D. 470–543), an eminent jurist and friend of Justinian. The four segments of this massive effort later became known as the *Corpus juris civilis*, and served to preserve and revitalize the old Roman law. Justinian's legal reforms and the *Corpus juris civilis* shaped the development of both civil and ecclesiastical law throughout Europe for many centuries. They continue to influence the legal thought of the civil law system today.

The church of San Vitale (St. Vitalis) in Ravenna, Italy, was consecrated by Archbishop Maximian in A.D. 547. Its mosaics, created at Justinian's command by artists from Constantinople, are among the finest in a city known for its superb mosaics. Justinian wanted to be seen as the sole legitimate sovereign, as the man chosen by God to rule the empire. In a huge mosaic over the apse, he is shown with members of his court offering a golden bowl to Christ, who appears on the ceiling (not pictured here). On either side of Justinian are the Archbishop Maximian and General Belisarius. For Justinian, Belisarius had reconquered much of North Africa, southern Spain, Italy, and Sicily.

On an adjacent section of the apse, also not in this illustration, is Justinian's wife and collaborator, the Empress Theodora, with her court. Theodora shared in Justinian's power to an unusual

degree for that time and was empress in her own right, not merely the emperor's consort. She died in 547, the year the church of San Vitale was consecrated. Because both Theodora and Justinian are shown with halos it is doubted by some scholars that the mosaics were completed during their lifetimes.

Colorplate 6. Mosaic. Basilica of San Vitale, Ravenna. Scala/Art Resource, NY.

ca. 1770

Ch'Ang Hsiu

Confucius (or K'ung-fu-tzu; 551–479 B.C.), the great Chinese sage and teacher, was also a travelling magistrate who viewed law within a larger framework of social order. Law was only one of the forces that were needed in governing society and clearly it was neither the best, nor the most important. One saying attributed to Confucius reflects his conviction that moral persuasion should come before legal controls: "As a judge, I decide disputes, for that is my duty; but the best thing that could happen would be to eliminate the causes for litigation!"

Confucius served in several bureaucratic posts before becoming a teacher, and believed that one of the goals of education was enlightened public service. Although he favored making education broadly available, he saw the training of the nobility as its major function. Later in his life, he held higher posts including that of minister of justice in his province of Lu, but become disenchanted and left public life at the age of fifty-six for a twelve-year, self-imposed exile.

The political philosophy which Confucius sought to convey (and he saw himself as a transmitter or teacher, not as an innovator) was conservative and feudal. It was based on a government of men, rather than of laws. A good ruler, an enlightened and moral nobility, ritual observance, and family ties were more important to society than the protection offered by legal texts. Conciliation and compromise were the preferred means of dispute resolution. Natural law and a natural order of the world, based on the harmonious adjustment of all its parts, was the underlying theory.

This view of the world, and of people's roles in it, was developed and embodied by later disciples of Confucius in the *Analects*, the sacred scriptures of Confucianism. This tradition, despite relative decline in some periods, has had a remarkably sustained continuity throughout Chinese history. It influenced philosophy, religion, government, law, the arts, and all areas of human endeavor, not only in China itself but throughout East Asia, until the middle of this century.

Countermovements developed in China at times, but usually only for brief periods. For example, in the two centuries immediately following Confucius, another school, appropriately called the Legists, held sway. Those philosophers favored the concept of a government of laws, not men, and they effectively shaped the social structure and the bureaucracy accordingly. Their dominance ended, however, and Confucianism was restored. It remains to be seen whether the old tradition will arise again to replace the Marxism of the present Chinese regime. Although the teaching of Confucius has been a primary ideological anathema during the cultural revolution of recent years, there is evidence that the teaching of the ancient magistrate survives as a subtle force in Chinese life and thought today.

Colorplate 7. From an album of portraits of well-known Chinese. Gouache on paper. 13 3/16 × 8" (33.5 × 20.2 cm). Bibliothèque Nationale, Paris.

至聖孔子

名丘字仲尼山東
兗州府曲阜縣人

Late eighteenth century

Jacques-Louis David

Jacques-Louis David's painting, *The Trial of Phryne*, is another example of the French revolutionary artist's interest in the defiance of authority[1] as a subject for his art. Phryne, a Greek courtesan of the fourth-century B.C., had wealth, wit, and great beauty. Because of these attractive qualities and her general notoriety, she became the subject of many anecdotes and legends. It was said, for example, that Phryne had offered to rebuild the walls of Thebes destroyed by Alexander the Great. Her condition, however, was that the restoration be inscribed: "Destroyed by Alexander, restored by Phryne, the courtesan."

Phryne was accused of blasphemy in profaning the Eleusinian mysteries and brought to trial for that capital offense. The Eleusinian mysteries held in the town of Eleusis near Athens, were religious rites that celebrated the rescue by Demeter, the goddess of agriculture and fertility, of her daughter, Persephone, who had been abducted by Hades to the lower worlds. The rites symbolized faith in the renewal and continuance of life, and may have been enhanced by the use of sacred hallucinogenic mushrooms, the "food of the Gods." The visions, thoughts, and experience which resulted were among the secrets and mysteries protected by threat of the death penalty.

The prosecution of Phryne is but one example in a long history of the law's use to enforce or protect religious interests. This instance may have been provoked by an incident during a festival at Eleusis, when Phryne took off her clothes, let down her hair, and entered the sea in full view of the people. At her trial, Phryne was defended by Hyperides (390–322 B.C.), an Athenian orator and military leader who was also one of her lovers. When Hyperides realized that the evidence against Phryne was overwhelming and that she would be convicted, he tore open her robe, displaying her breasts. An alternative version has Phryne baring herself and pleading directly for her life. In any case, the court was so moved by her naked beauty that she was acquitted. Praxiteles, the foremost sculptor of that time, made a statue of Phryne which was placed next to one of Aphrodite (also by him) in a temple at Thespiae.

This painting by David is one of the many he based on ancient history and mythology. A number of those, including this dramatic scene, reflect the impact in classical literature of either romantic love or erotic passion. Sex in the courtroom has been a common theme in both art and literature.

1. For other examples here, see *The Death of Socrates* (page 20) and the *Tennis Court Oath* (page 72). It should be noted that, after his election to the Revolutionary Convention in 1792, David successfully defended two French artists who were being persecuted by the Inquisition in Rome.

Colorplate 8. Oil on canvas. 57 × 78⅞" (145 × 195 cm). Musée's département aux de Loin-Atlantique, Musée Dobrée, Nantes. Ch. Hémon Collection.

1882–1888

Cesare Maccari

In ancient Rome, skillful oratory was a quality of major political and legal importance, and brought great respect and admiration to those who possessed it. Marcus Tullius Cicero (106–43 B.C.), philosopher, lawyer, and republican politician, was perhaps the most renowned of the Roman orators. He spoke in the Senate and to the people in the forum on public matters, and in the courts as a lawyer, most often as defendant's counsel in criminal cases. Fifty-eight of his approximately one hundred six speeches survive, along with several of his books on oratory and rhetoric.

Cicero served as praetor (an annually elected magistrate) in 66 B.C., and was chosen as consul for 63 B.C. Consuls were the two chief magistrates of the republic, elected annually. He opposed Caesar's dictatorship, but was not a party to his murder in 44. Cicero was ultimately slain in the conflict that followed Caesar's assassination, and was considered by many to be a martyr to the republican cause.

Among his most famous orations were four speeches, in the Senate and in the forum, against Lucius Sergius Catilina (108–62 B.C.), known as Catiline, and his fellow conspirators. Cicero had ample basis for his enmity toward Catiline, an aristocrat turned revolutionary demagogue. Catiline was rumored to have murdered his own brother-in-law and was said to have compromised Fabia, a vestal virgin who was the half-sister of Cicero's wife. Catiline's radical ideas favoring the poor against the wealthy (e.g., cancellation of all debts) were anathema to the conservative Cicero. They were also rivals for the consulship to which Cicero was appointed. During Cicero's consulship, Catiline led a secret conspiracy to seize control of the government. The coup failed in part because informers had kept Cicero advised of its plans, which he promptly thwarted.

Catiline then prepared for open war, and made an unsuccessful attempt to murder Cicero in his home. In the Senate, on the next day, Cicero delivered his first oration against the insurrection, forcing Catiline to retreat. Cicero then aroused the people in the forum with the second oration, and, as a result, the conspirators were declared public enemies, and an army was sent against them. One group was arrested, convicted, and executed in 63, having been incriminated by evidence which Cicero had collected. The following year, Catiline himself was slain in battle in a total military defeat. Some find it ironic that Cicero himself was to die in a somewhat parallel opposition to the Triumvirate who ruled after Caesar's death.

This painting of one of Cicero's orations against Catiline was executed between 1882 and 1888 by a minor Italian artist, Cesare Maccari. It reflects a period in which Italian painters were much influenced by photography and a new realistic style. It strikingly portrays the antagonism between the two dominant actors—eloquent Cicero and brooding Catiline—thereby conveying the part played by strong individuals in both law and history. The scene also illustrates the role of the Roman Senate (and perhaps future legislatures) in protecting public order and preserving the integrity of government itself.

Colorplate 9. Oil on canvas. Villa Madama, Rome. Scala/Art Resource, NY.

GREGORY IX RECEIVING DECRETALS FROM RAYMOND DA PEÑA FORTE

1512

Raphael

Gregory IX (1145–1241), originally Ugoline of Segni, was pope of the Roman Catholic church from 1227 to 1241. He was a vigorous leader and an active defender of papal prerogatives, an influential canon lawyer, and a theologian of note. An experienced diplomat and a forceful political figure, Gregory was an austere but decisive man, with a harsh personality and a volatile temper. He used his temporal power aggressively, and was in frequent conflict with Emperor Frederick II.

As pope, Gregory had great impact on the Church and on the Western world, not only in his day, but in the centuries that followed. That influence was felt in many fields and flowed from a variety of achievements. Gregory helped draft the rule of the Franciscan order; he assisted in the revival of Aristotelian philosophy; and he founded the Papal Inquisition. Perhaps his major accomplishment was the commissioning and proclamation (in 1234) of the five books of the *Decretals*, the second great foundation of the canon law.

Canon law not only specified the organization, governance, and discipline of the Christian church, but also shaped much of what is now secular life. It strongly influenced domestic relations, crime and punishment, property and succession, evidence and procedure, and international law. It also served to preserve and transmit Roman law to modern times and, in turn, shaped the development of the civil law system that predominates in much of the world today.

The vast and disorganized accumulation of Church legislation and papal decisions over the centuries was systematically digested by an Italian monk, Gratian, at the University of Bologna in 1140. The resulting compilation, called the *Decretum of Gratian*, included approximately four thousand canon law documents and virtually established the canon law as a system which could be taught and applied.

Raymond of Peña Forte (ca. 1175–ca. 1240) was a Dominican canonist, a professor at Bologna, and one of the judges of the Rota, the Church's Supreme Court. From 1230 to 1234, by order of Gregory IX, Raymond prepared a supplementary collection of papal decretals and constitutions. Known as the *Decretals of Gregory IX*, this compilation was proclaimed by Pope Gregory in 1234 and came to form the fifth book of the *Corpus juris canonici*.

Gregory's reception of the decretals from Raymond is portrayed here in a fresco, painted by Raphael in 1512 under commission from Pope Julius II as part of the overall redecoration of the papal apartments in the Vatican. Pope Julius II, who ruled from 1503 to 1513, was in fact the model for Gregory in this work. The decoration included medallions of female figures, representing theology, law, poetry, and philosophy. (See Raphael's *Justice*, page 54.) These symbolized all of Western learning of that time and the four branches of knowledge and wisdom needed by a pope. The painting of Gregory and his decretals adorned the papal signature room.

Raphael (1483–1520) of Urbino was one of the great painters of the Italian Renaissance. This painting, done during his Roman period when he was at the height of his genius, was stimulated by the work of Michelangelo and other contemporary luminaries. Its clarity and architectural splendor enhance the drama of the historic lawgiving.

Colorplate 10. The Justice Wall in the Stanza della Segnatura. Fresco. The Vatican, Rome. Scala Art Resource, NY.

ca. 1300–1315

The *Mirror of Saxony* or *Sachsenspiegel* was a code of customary law written about 1230 in Latin by Eike von Repkow, a knight and lay-judge (*schoeffen*) of East-Phalia in Saxony. It is one of the earliest Germanic legal texts and was particularly popular after being translated into German. Its influence extended beyond its immediate place and time. Similar works of local law, some of which were based at least in part on the *Sachsenspiegel*, appeared throughout western Europe in the thirteenth century. The French *Coutumes* (pages 38 and 44) of the thirteenth century were a parallel form of legal text. The *Sachsenspiegel* continued to be a significant legal source even into the twentieth century.

The *Mirror of Saxony*, which contained *landrecht* (general or territorial law) and *lehnrecht* (feudal law), was accorded the status of statute law in the courts of Saxony. Although its genre reflected a period of localization in law, the development of similarities among the *Mirrors* of various localities reflected the beginnings of French and German common law. There were the *Mirror of Swabia* or *Schwabenspiegel* (ca. 1275); *Mirror of Justices*, prepared in London in law French around 1285; a Dutch *Sachsenspiegel*; and many others. While these texts or codes were typically based on the ancient law of the locale, feudal and manorial in nature, they also contained an infusion of Roman and canon law, and often royal legislation and decrees.

The compilations created (or reflected the prior existence of) local courts with lay-judges, presided over by the local ruler or his sheriff. The proceedings were generally held outdoors, or in open-sided courtrooms to assure public notice. Formal oath giving was an important part of the procedure, with the accused (or both parties to a civil dispute) giving an oath, along with supporting oaths from relatives, friends, or other compurgators. This method of fact-finding is considered by some to be a precursor of the use of juries.

Many of the manuscripts of the *Sachenspiegel* were brilliantly illuminated, as was this one from Heidelberg, done between 1300 and 1315. The illustration here shows twenty-one oath givers in support of a litigant being questioned by the official presiding over the trial. This early illustrated text of the *Mirror of Saxony* has survived in four copies, known as the Dresden, Heidelberg, Oldenburg, and Wolfenbüttel manuscripts. The use of explanatory pictures alongside the text, facilitating instruction in the content and use of these compilations, may have been an early form of visual aid in legal education.

Colorplate 11. Illuminated manuscript. Parchment. 11¹³/₁₆ × 9¹/₄" (30 × 23.5 cm). Universitätsbibliothek, Heidelberg.

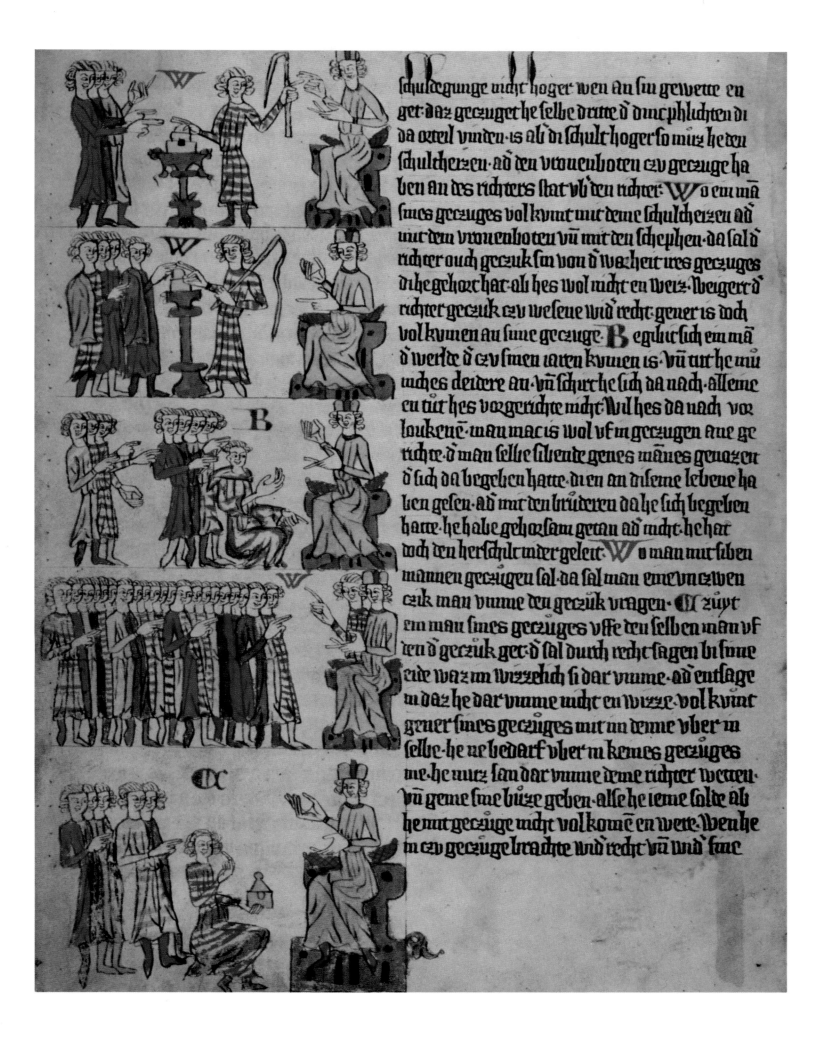

schuldegunge nicht hoger wen an sin gewette en
get. daz gezuget he selbe dritte oder dincphluchten di
da orteil vinden is ab di schult hoger so mut he den
schultheizen add den vrouenboten ezu gezuge ha
ben an des richters stat vb den richter. Wo em man
sines gezuges vol kumt mit deme schultheizen add
mit den vrouenboten vn mit den schephen. da sal der
richter ouch gezuk sin von der warheit ires gezuges
di he gehort hat. ab hes wol nicht en weiz. weigert der
richter gezuk ezu wesene vn rechtt gener is doch
vol kumen an sine gezuge. Begitlich em man
der werde der ezu sinen iaren kumen is. vn tut he mu
nches deidere an. vn schure sich da nach. alleine
en tut hes vorgerichte nicht. Wil hes da nach vor
loukene. man macis wol vf in gezugen ane ge
richte der man selbe silvende genes manues genazet
der sich da begeben hatte. di en an disene lebene ha
ben gesen. add mit den bruderen da he sich begeben
hatte. he habe gehorsam getan add nicht. he hat
doch den herschilt nider geleit. Wo man mit siben
mannen gezugen sal. da sal man eneun czwen
czik man vmme den gezuk vragen. Ol zuyt
em man sines gezuges vffe den selben man vf
ten der gezuk get der sal durch rechtt sagen bi sine
eide waz in wizzelich si dar vmme. add entsage
in daz he dar vmme nicht en wizze. vol kumt
gener sines gezuges mit un deme vber in
selbe. he ne bedarf vber in kemes gezuges
me. he mut san dar vmme deme richter wetten
vn gene sine buze geben. alse he ieme solde ab
he mit gezuge nicht volkome en were. Wen he
in ezu gezuge brachte und rechtt vn und sine

Before 1268

Attributed to Hendry de Bracton

Henry de Bracton (or Bratton), who died in 1268, is credited with the first systematic treatise on English law—*De legibus et consuetudinibus Angliae* (*On the Laws and Customs of England*), written in Latin after 1250. The unorganized accumulation of legal decisions and pleadings from English courts in the centuries following the Norman Conquest impeded the development of the common law system. There was need for a systematic statement synthesizing the multitude of individual cases and rulings. Bracton's work, based on his observation of many cases during his long years as a judge, was designed to meet that need.

A previous treatise, also in Latin, completed between 1187 and 1189 and credited to Ranulph de Glanvill, *Tractatus de legibus et consuetudinibus Angliae* (*Treatise on the Laws and Customs of England*), provided an earlier statement of legal procedure in the royal courts. It remained for Bracton, a cleric who, after learning law, became an itinerant justice and later a judge of the King's Bench, to provide a broader, more thorough, and more systematic summary. Although ten times the length of Glanvill's text, Bracton's also focused largely on practice and procedure. Parts of it showed the influences of Roman and canon law on the developing English law.

After circulating in numerous manuscripts (forty-nine of which are known to survive) for three hundred years, Bracton's treatise was finally printed in 1569. An inadequate translation into English was done in the late nineteenth century, and an excellent one completed in four volumes by Professor Samuel Thorne in 1968–77. As with the contemporaneous French and German collections, some of the Bracton manuscripts were beautifully illuminated and illustrated, like the one shown here. Also, like its continental counterparts, Bracton's exposition significantly influenced subsequent centuries of legal development.

Bracton's statement of his purpose in preparing the treatise is both a reflection of the legal system for which it was written and a classic contemporary comment on the role of scholarship in the administration of justice:

"Since, however, laws and customs of this kind are often abusively perverted by the foolish and unlearned (who ascend the judgment-seat before they have learnt the laws), and those who are involved in doubts and conjectures are very frequently led astray by their elders, who decide causes rather according to their own pleasure than by the authority of the laws, I, Henry de Bracton, have, for the instruction, at least of the younger generation, undertaken the task of diligently examining the ancient judgments of righteous men, not without much loss of sleep and labour, and by reducing their acts, counsels, and answers, and whatever thereof

I have found noteworthy into one summary, I have brought it into order under titles and paragraphs . . . to be commended to perpetual memory by the aid of writing. . . ."[1]

By providing a reliable statement of English practice and procedure and a useable summary of the case law up to that time, Bracton aided the king's judges in their efforts to unify and develop the customary law of the realm.

1. R. Pound and T. F. T. Plucknett, *Readings in the History of the Common Law*, 3d ed. (Rochester, NY: Lawyers Co-operative Publishing Co., 1927), 127–128.

Colorplate 12. Manuscript text. Parchment. British Library, London.

Courtroom Scene,
From *Le Coutume de Normandie*

1450–1470

Customary law consists of bodies of customs and practices which become so accepted in a particular region that they are recognized as law and are enforced by local tribunals. During the medieval period, life in much of Europe was regulated by some form of customary law, except where the revival of Roman law had supplanted it.

As people settled into an agricultural life, feudal rules linked them to the land and encouraged the development of local customary law. The customs and usages of each locality, and the bodies of law that grew out of them, were territorial in nature and therefore binding on all the inhabitants of that area. In the thirteenth and fourteenth centuries, many of these local collections of customary law were recorded and codified. Such manuscripts were copied and distributed, and strengthened the local legal systems in their resistance to the Roman law that was spreading through Europe.

In France, where different bodies of law dominated in the country's several regions, these collections of local law, called *coutumes*, were strongest in the central and northern regions. Local parliaments, more often judicial than legislative, decided cases on the basis of the local customary law as embodied in their coutume. The parliaments were thus able to resist the development of a common law for all of France.

In the fifteenth century, the collecting and recording of coutumes became more centralized, first by province, and then as a national effort ordered by Charles VII in 1453. By the time of the French Revolution, there were still sixty provincial coutumes and three hundred local collections. The final version of the coutumes for each area underwent a process of local approval and, when adopted by the local parliament, acquired the force of statutory law. The coutumes were a major source for the codification of law under Napoleon, and they remain a primary source of law in France today. Their influence was carried to Louisiana through the *Code Napoleon* and through the use of other French legal sources in that civil law state.

The illustration shown here is from an illuminated manuscript of the *Coutume de Normandie*, written between 1450 and 1470. It derives from the second major compilation of Norman law, the *Grand coutumier de Normandie*, compiled between 1254 and 1258. Because of the close historical links between Normandy and England, the coutumes of Normandy were in some respects closer to English law than to other French coutumes. The unique regional character of Norman law continued at least to the Revolution.

The illustration shows twelve local men meeting with judges to decide a case. This early form of fact finding is related to the parallel development of the common law jury system in England and to the oath givers described in the *Mirror of Saxony* (page 34).

Colorplate 13. Illustrated manuscript. 6¾ × 4¾" (16.8 × 12.2 cm). Rare Book Collection, Law Library, Library of Congress, Washington, D.C.

38

ALLEGORY OF GOOD GOVERNMENT

1338–1340

Ambrogio Lorenzetti

As the ancient Egyptians personified justice in the goddess Maat (page 14), so the ancient Greeks and Romans followed with their own representations of this important concept. The Greeks created symbols of justice in the goddess Themis and her daughter Dike. Themis, second wife of Zeus, presided with him over law and order, and represented divine justice. Her daughter Dike, one of the Horae, or goddesses of order in nature, was also a goddess of justice. Dike was said to have informed Zeus of unjust judicial decisions so that he could punish their perpetrators.

In Roman mythology, the figure of justice is again female, but is called Justitia, and is usually shown with scales and often with a cornucopia as well. Later, in Christian art, Justitia appears in a variety of styles[1]—sometimes with a halo, sometimes with a blindfold, sometimes with a sword, or with some combination of them. In the Middle Ages, she is often shown as one of the four Cardinal Virtues, along with Fortitude, Prudence, and Temperance.

The female figure of justice is still very much with us today. She appears frequently in and on our public buildings, particularly courthouses, as a reminder, an encouragement, or a warning of the ideal to be pursued. Over the last two thousand years, the mood and message of this figure has varied with the needs of the time, the intent of her sponsors, and the prevailing ethos. One of the richest and most complex representations is that executed during 1338–1340 by Ambrogio Lorenzetti (ca. 1290s–1348). It appears in frescoes at the town hall (*Palazzo Publico*) of Siena, Italy.

The frescoes, which became known as *Good and Bad Government*, consist of large rectangular panels in the former hall of the magistrates who ruled Siena from 1287 to 1355. One of the panels, called *Allegory of Good Government*, includes the image of justice shown here. The scene, reflecting the political theology of St. Thomas Aquinas, was intended to glorify the commune of Siena as the embodiment of government based on the common good rather than on private interests.

Justice, sitting on her throne, looks up to heaven, toward a small winged figure of wisdom holding a pair of scales that, in turn, are supported by the hands of Justice. In the pans of the scales are two angels who dispense distributive justice (on the left) and commutative justice (on the right). Distributive Justice crowns one person and beheads another, while commutative Justice seems to give money to one and arms to another. Below Justice is another female figure, Concord, who holds cords attached to the scales and transmits them to a group of citizens, probably the founders of the Sienese government.

This elaborate allegory is a far cry from the simpler figures of justice in today's courtrooms. It seems to combine the *legal* functions of justice (reward and punishment) with the *civic* functions (regulating social, economic, and political activities). The scene reflects a humanistic concept of justice and an artist deeply concerned with issues of moral and political philosophy. Ambrogio was, in fact, such an individual—well educated, a student of classical art, and a thinker of curiosity and originality. By relating justice to the more general concept of good government, he has added another dimension to the image of law in art.

1. For a survey of these forms, with a modern interpretation, see D. E. Curtis and J. Resnik, "Images of Justice," *Yale Law Journal* 96(1987): 1727–1772.

Colorplate 14. Detail. Fresco. Town Hall, Siena.

CONJUGAL LAW: ADULTEROUS WIFE APPEARING IN COURT

Fifteenth century

Historically, the role of women in the law and in the courts has more often been that of victim than victor. Traditional stories of women who have survived difficult, and often unjust, prosecutions have been celebrated in art and literature. Phryne (page 28), and Susanna in the story of Susanna and the Elders from the *Apocrypha*, are examples of heroines who were vindicated at the bar. More frequent, however, were the cases of women who lost their trials, such as Joan of Arc (page 52) and Katharine of Aragon (page 56), and were martyred as a result.

Although women of the upper classes enjoyed a relatively high status in some ancient civilizations (particularly in Egypt), in others (like Rome) they were subordinated to their male relatives or spouses. In early Christianity and through the Renaissance in Europe their legal status remained depressed. Although there was some relief following the French Revolution, it was not until the second half of the nineteenth century that women began to secure equal property rights. Full political rights were not won in most countries until the twentieth century.

Most women who were so unfortunate as to be summoned to court as defendants could expect an unsympathetic hearing. Often, the very process of proving one's innocence was itself a substantial punishment. The accusation of witchcraft, or any hint of witchcraft in connection with another allegation of wrongdoing, was often fatal, even without significant proof. This was particularly true under inquisitorial systems which not only lacked a presumption of innocence, but also often put the burden of disproving the accusation on the defendant.

The legal disabilities suffered by women were particularly heavy when the charge was related to the marital relationship. Such rights as a single woman might have enjoyed at various times and places were frequently subordinated to her husband's interests when she married. The differential treatment of an adulterous partner to a marriage, depending on whether the husband or the wife was found guilty, was a noteworthy example. Adultery was in any case a serious offense, and under some circumstances was punishable by death under Greek, Roman, Mosaic, canon law, for long periods in English law, and even in the early law of colonial Massachusetts. Even when capital punishment was not imposed, the penalty for women was likely to be disproportionately harsh.

One modern writer describes these punishments as follows:

> "Adultery on the part of the woman was cruelly penalized in this world, and she was eternally damned in the next. The catalogue of her punishments is a long one. . . . She was imprisoned, ostracized, stoned with stones that she die, poisoned, persecuted, bedeviled, robbed of her children, starved in dungeons, flagellated, driven naked through the streets, banished to deserts; and she was forced into prostitution. Briefly, for this offense she has been subjected to every fiendish torture that savage cruelty could invent or wickedness devise. . . ."[1]

The charge or suspicion of adultery is a frequent literary theme. It figures prominently in Chaucer's *Canterbury Tales*; in Shakespeare's *Othello*; in Hawthorne's *The Scarlet Letter*; and in more modern novels and plays than we can count.

The illuminated fifteenth-century, Spanish manuscript, shown here, illustrates such a legal proceeding against a wife for adultery.

1. Ralcy Husted Bell, *Some Aspects of Adultery: A Study*. (NY: Eugenics Publishing Company, 1933).

Colorplate 15. Manuscript. Royal Library, El Escorial. Giraudon/ Art Resource, NY.

Ermimisi
mo testnu'
prum. nomen.
ignatio tex
ego. bisp ug dx
tto conlebes
lib um num
uixtentibs
sinti quen

A WAGER OF BATTEL,
FROM *LE COUTUME DE NORMANDIE*

1450–1470

In many ancient cultures, legal disputes were settled by a variety of physical tests, such as subjecting the accused to a painful ordeal and, later, to different duel-like forms of judicial combat. These methods continued in many parts of Europe through the Middle Ages. The ordeal was condemned by the Fourth Lateran Council in 1215 and died out gradually thereafter, but trial by battle continued in some areas, even into the Renaissance.

Judicial duels were used to decide both civil disputes and criminal trials, and were based on the assumption that the result was determined by divine intervention, not merely by the strength or endurance of the parties involved. God would decide the issue by favoring the truthful or innocent party. The Church often used the procedure in its own property disputes, although priests (along with women, infants, and the aged) could avoid personal participation by selecting a champion to appear on their behalf.

The judicial duels known as wagers of battle are generally considered to be Teutonic in origin, and to have spread from the German tribes to France and then throughout Europe. An edict in Lyons in A.D. 501 recognized the wager of battle as an accepted trial procedure, and it was used widely in France where its rules were documented in the coutumes. Trial by battle was introduced into England by William the Conqueror and flourished there as well. Initially, it was only compulsory when both parties were Normans; later, it was imposed generally. Several examples occur in Shakespeare's plays (e.g., the opening scene of *Richard II*). There are evidences of such trials in Elizabethan England and one aborted incident as late as 1817. The practice was finally abolished by Parliament in 1819.

In England the wager of battle was usually held before the judges of the Court of Queen's Bench or the Court of Common Pleas. The parties fought with a staff and a shield, until one party gave up. If neither yielded by the time the stars came out, the defendant was considered the victor. The French version shown here in the

Grand coutumier de Normandie manuscript (1450–1470) is understandably similar, considering the affinity between English and Norman law. The Library of Congress describes this proceeding, as follows[1]:

> "When a plaintiff's accusations were denied by the defendant, the case often had to be settled by duel. At noon on the appointed day, four *chevalliers* took the two *champions* to a *champ*. After an elaborate, prescribed ritual of prayers and oaths, the opponents fought. 'Se le deffédeur poeut deffendre soy tant que les estoilles pairent au ciel Il aura vaicu la partie. . . .' [If the defendant can defend himself until two stars appear in the sky, he will be victorious over his opponent.] In this miniature, evenly spaced, five-pointed gold stars stud the darkening sky."

Montesquieu in book 28 of *The Spirit of Laws* (1748) described the rules and procedures for judicial combat. He suggested that while there were many wise things conducted in a foolish manner, this was an example of a foolish thing conducted in a wise manner.

1. J. Carswell and I. Sipkov, *The Coutumes of France in the Library of Congress: An Annotated Bibliography* (Washington: Library of Congress, 1977), [40].

Colorplate 16. Illuminated manuscript. 6¾ × 4¾" (16.8 × 12.2 cm). Rare Book Collection, Law Library, Library of Congress, Washington, D.C.

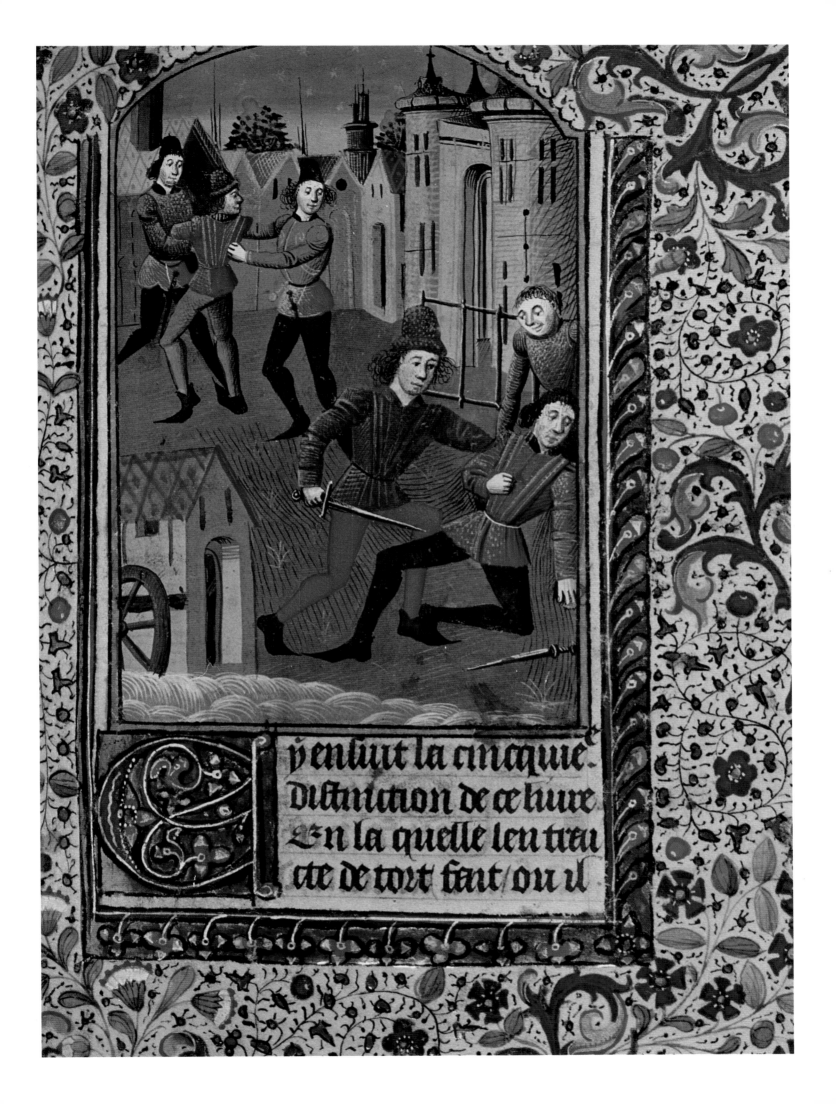

p enfuit la cincquie
diftinction de ce liure
en la quelle len trai
cte de tort fait / ou il

The origins of the modern university are generally agreed to be in the twelfth century, particularly in Bologna and Paris. These developments were undoubtedly stimulated by the infusion of new learning and the revival of old texts. The Roman law of Justinian, virtually dormant for centuries, was reborn from a few surviving manuscripts and from elementary forms that had been preserved in the customary law of Rome.

The revival of Roman law in Bologna was aided by the work of several distinguished scholars and teachers. The first of these, a doctor of law, known only as Pepo (ca. 1076), lectured at Bologna and is referred to in legal documents in the last quarter of the eleventh century. Better known was Irnerius (ca. 1070–1138), who lectured on Justinian's code and digest at Bologna and developed the method of "glossing" legal texts. Irnerius attracted students from all over Europe and is credited with establishing law as a subject of professional and scholarly study. His popularity and prestige contributed directly to making Bologna the major center of learning in Europe, thereby leading to the founding there of Europe's first university.

Around 1140, Gratian (ca. 1090–1159), a monk from Ravenna, came to Bologna and compiled the *Decretum*, the collection of texts (page 32) widely accepted as the standard canon law compilation.

Another early legal scholar was Azo (ca. 1150–1230), a professor of civil law at Bologna and one of the leading glossators on the texts of Roman law. His work influenced Bracton (page 36) and other scholars and contemporary judges. Law study was pursued as well as Padua, Perugia, Ravenna, and other Italian cities, and spread gradually throughout western Europe.

Bologna and most of the other early universities were largely controlled by the students who hired, paid, and discharged their teachers. The professors, however, controlled the awarding of diplomas which, in effect, were admissions to the guilds of doctors. The students organized into national groups and were in frequent conflict with

say the university in Bologna was organized by the students as a means of protection against high

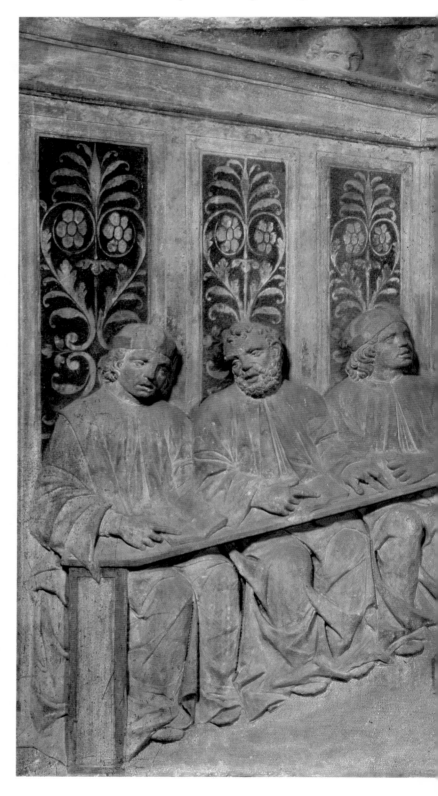

both their professors and the townspeople. Some prices for rooms and other necessities.

The illustration here, *Law Lecturer and His Class*, is a detail of the frieze on the marble sarcophagus of Pietro Canonici, a lecturer on civil law at Bologna. From the fifteenth century, it is now in the Civic Museum at Bologna.

Colorplate 17. Detail of a sarcophagus frieze. Marble. Museo Civico, Bologna. Scala/Art Resource, NY.

ca. 1500

The unification of law and of the legal system was not achieved in France until long after that centralization occurred in England. The power of feudal rulers and their courts, the durability of local and regional coutumes (page 38), and the effectiveness of provincial parlements impeded the development of a uniform body of law by the royal courts. However, centralization of authority was impossible without a unified legal system and laws of general applicability.

In the thirteenth and fourteenth centuries, the French kings sought to strengthen and centralize their authority. In the thirteenth century, this included the creation of new royal judicial officers, the *baillis* or *sénéchals*, with both original and appellate jurisdiction. At the same time, the Parliament of Paris began to develop out of the Curia Regis, combining important judicial responsibilities with legislative functions. It usually sat in Paris, but had jurisdiction over a much wider area. The number of judges assigned to its judicial functions grew steadily until 1345 when the number settled at about eighty, many times that of the comparable English courts. By the fifteenth century the workload had become so heavy that provincial parliaments were established following the structure and procedures of the Paris model.

The judges were largely drawn from the clergy because of their training in canon law and their familiarity with Roman Law. Roughly half of the Parliament's judicial officers were clerics, including even archbishops and bishops who sat on a temporary basis. Unlike the vastly diminished power and prestige of the French judiciary *after* the Revolution, judges in the royal service in earlier periods were highly reputed, well rewarded, and generally well educated. From the middle of the fourteenth century, it was a mark of their status that the officers of Parliament were given an increasing role in the selection of its judges.

The judges gradually developed many of the powers and subsidiary functions that we associate with a modern court. They regulated and disciplined the lawyers who practiced before them;

prepared rules and forms of procedure; arranged for the collection of evidence in areas distant from the court; recorded their decisions and arranged for their publication; and at times even claimed the right to deviate from existing law. By the sixteenth century, the royal judges, through their decisions, were beginning to unify French private law, while the growing acceptance of royal legislation was unifying public law.

This illustration from a compendium of the Ordinances of the City of Paris (ca. 1500) shows the following different legal functionaries performing their duties before a panel of judges: *procureur* (state's attorney); *gresse* (registrar); *receueur* (cashier); and *clerc* (clerk).

Colorplate 18. Bibliothéque de l'Arsenal, Paris. Giraudon/Art Resource, NY.

1531

The *audiencia* was a court established in late medieval Spain to administer royal justice. In the sixteenth century, *audiencias* were created in the colonial districts of Spanish America. They were empowered to hear and resolve complaints against colonial officials, to restrain local abuses of power, and to protect the rights of the local inhabitants. They had both civil and criminal jurisdiction, and the *audiencia* of Mexico had jurisdiction over all of Mexico, the Gulf Coast, and Florida.

After his conquest of Mexico, Hernando Cortes (1485–1547) came into conflict with the *First Audiencia of New Spain*, sitting in Tenochtitlán (now Mexico City). The Spanish authorities had introduced a system of rewarding favored colonists or conquistadors with *encomienda*, grants of the labor of the natives. This resulted of course in the involuntary servitude of the local population, many of whom died as a result. In return for these grants, the colonists were supposed to protect and convert the Indians, and to provide military service to defend the colony.

Cortes took for himself an enormous number of such forced laborers whom he refused to give up when *encomienda* were later forbidden. Such excesses and the irregularity of his military operations made him many enemies both in Spain and in the Americas. As a result, Cortes was deposed in 1528, and in response he brought a lawsuit against the *audiencia* in 1528.

The *Huejotzingo Codex*, shown here, was a manuscript containing testimony in the case, favorable to Cortes, from the Aztec community of Huejotzing. The *Codex* consists of eight native paintings on local leaf paper. They list the costs incurred by the Indians for food and materials in construction work they performed, records of tribute they paid to the royal treasury, and details of their labors. The documents functioned as depositions, in a pictorial form. The judgment went against the *audiencia*, and was appealed, but the result of the appeal is uncertain.

At about this time, Cortes went back to Spain to make a personal appeal to the emperor against the restraints on his activities in Mexico. He was received with distinction and given new titles, but when he returned to Mexico, his authority was reduced. A viceroy was appointed to administer civil affairs, and Cortes was left with only military authority. That division of power perpetuated tensions between Cortes and his enemies. This litigation illustrated the operation of colonial justice in New Spain, which had little apparent effect on the calamities that the Spanish conquest brought to the local inhabitants.

Colorplate 19. Manuscript. Harkness Collection, Library of Congress, Washington, D.C.

JOAN OF ARC AT THE CORONATION OF CHARLES VII

1851–1854

Jean August Dominique Ingres

J oan of Arc (1412–1431), the peasant girl who became both a saint and the national heroine of France, was the defendant in one of the most dramatic political trials in history. Although nominally a religious trial conducted by the Church, its underlying purposes were as much secular as sacred. Joan's prosecution, conviction, and execution at the stake for heresy and witchcraft was the direct result of the war then raging between England and France, and the conflict between warring factions within a divided France.

When she was thirteen, Joan believed that she was instructed by God, through the voices of angels and saints, to aid the Dauphin (the uncrowned king of France, later to be Charles VII) in driving the English from France. The English, with many French collaborators, then occupied much of France and were besieging Orléans. After long interrogation by theologians favorable to the Dauphin and much persuasion, Joan obtained his consent and support to fight the English. She then raised and led a small army and lifted the siege of Orléans against overwhelming English forces. Despite that triumph and a series of other military victories, Joan had difficulty persuading Charles to go to Reims and be crowned king of France. Finally, he and his ever-hesitant advisors agreed, and he was crowned at Reims on July 17, 1429, with Joan in attendance.

Further military success, however, was followed by defeats, and Joan was captured on May 23, 1430, by Burgundy forces allied to the English. On several occasions she attempted to escape and Charles, then seeking a truce with the Duke of Burgundy, made no attempt to rescue her. After six months of imprisonment and harsh questioning, she was sold to the English and their allies, and tried by French inquisitors at Rouen in 1431. Her unorthodox beliefs and her direct communications from God had brought her into conflict with the Church; her conviction would also aid those who sought to discredit Charles by impeaching his coronation.

The long trial was conducted unfairly, and Joan was under frequent threat of torture. After her conviction, she was turned over to the secular authorities for execution on May 30, 1431, and was burned at the stake. Twenty years later, in 1450, Charles VII ordered an inquiry into the trial. Rehabilitation proceedings, held from 1455 to 1456, revoked the sentence and proclaimed her innocence. She was later honored by the French Revolution and, in 1803, by Napoleon who was then fighting the English. In 1920, Joan was canonized as a saint by Pope Benedict XV.

Jean August Dominique Ingres (1780–1867) painted *Joan of Arc at the Coronation of Charles VII* between 1851 and 1854. He was a pupil of Jacques-Louis David and his successor as leader of the classical movement in French painting. His expertise in drafting, his cold crystalline style, and his balanced composition, are all apparent in this portrait of Joan at the pinnacle of her fortunes. The face of the equerry at the left, behind the praying monk, is reputed to be a self-portrait of Ingres. The quotation on the tablet in the foreground has been translated as: "And in heaven, her stake is transformed into a throne." Long celebrated in art and literature, Joan appears here in an image which mixes intense piety with sensuous power.

Colorplate 20. Oil on canvas. 94½ × 70¾" (240 × 178 cm). Louvre, Paris. Giraudon/Arts Resource, NY.

ca. 1510
Raphael

In addition to painting historical scenes with legal themes, Raphael (1483–1520) also painted symbolic or allegorical figures of Justice, several of which were executed as part of the decoration of various rooms in the Vatican. One of the most appealing of these allegorical figures is *Justitia*, which appears in a fresco on the ceiling of the Stanza della Segnatura. Armed with a sword and the scales of justice, she is one of two representations of justice in the room. Also in the same room are two murals by Raphael: *Gregory IX Receiving the Decretals* (page 32) and *Justinian Delivering the Pandects to Trebonianus*. There is some question as to whether one or both of these were actually completed by Raphael.

The figure of Justice shown here appears in one of four ceiling medallions, on a background of imitation gold mosaic. Each medallion contains a young woman allegorically representing one of the following themes: theology, philosophy, poetry, and justice. The ceiling images relate to the subjects of the murals in the lower part of the room. One could interpret that relationship as moving from the abstract to the concrete; from the general to the specific; or from the heavenly ideal to its earthbound realization. The abstract concept of justice above is made concrete in the historical murals of *Pope Gregory* and *Justinian* on the walls below.

These decorations were commissioned by Pope Julius II for what originally was to be the library in his private Vatican apartments. The room was called the Stanza della Segnatura for the ecclesiastical court with that name which met there. Raphael may have modeled the dominance of his *Justitia* on the centrality of Justice in Lorenzetti's fresco, *Allegory of Good Government* (page 40). The external attributes of the two figures are, of course, very different, as is the overall composition and style of the two paintings. Raphael's fresco, completed around 1510, is a more modern image than the fourteenth century Lorenzetti representation. *Justicia* as painted by Raphael is graceful and beautiful, and conveys a sense of gentleness which is not easy to achieve for one waving a sword. A feeling that this depiction of Justice is softened by love or at least by nurture comes also from the four putti or cherubs that flank her.

The cherubs hold two tablets, with the inscription *Ius suum unicuique tribuit* (Render unto everyone his right). It is part of a sentence from the beginning of *Justinian's Digest* which states: "Justice is a steady and enduring will to render unto everyone his right."[1] It has been said that this *Justitia* "signifies not law, but the virtue of justice."[2] That notion somehow seems to be supported by the ambiguity inherent in the juxtaposition of sword and scales.

This fresco and Raphael's other works in the Stanza della Segnatura were done when he was at the height of his productivity and they brought him both fame and fortune.

1. *The Digest of Justinian*, translation edited by Alan Watson (Philadelphia: University of Pennsylvania Press, 1985, 1(bk.1, sec. 10): 2.

2. Mab van Lohuizen-Mulder, *Raphael's Images of Justice-Humanity-Friendship* (Wassenaar, The Netherlands: Mirananda, 1977), 144, note 144.

Colorplate 21. Fresco. The Vatican, Rome.

The Court for the Trial of Queen Katharine, from Shakespeare's *Henry VIII*, Act 2, Scene 4

ca. 1817

George Harlow

Katharine of Aragon (1485–1536), daughter of King Ferdinand and Queen Isabella of Spain, became the first wife of King Henry VIII, in 1509, after lengthy financial and political negotiations. Like most royal marriages of the time, this was a political alliance with military ramifications and fiscal considerations. Despite happy years together and Katharine's popularity in England, Henry, troubled by want of a male heir and by his desire for Anne Boleyn, sought to have the marriage annulled as incestuous. Before marrying Henry, Katharine had been married briefly to his older brother, Arthur, who had died five months later. That marriage was never consummated and hence was a nullity and no bar to Katharine's subsequent marriage to Henry.

Since marriage to one's brother-in-law was considered incestuous at that time, Henry raised the issue in order to free himself for a new marriage. He viewed Katharine's failure to produce a son as God's penalty for the illegality of their marriage. After several unsuccessful pregnancies, Katharine bore only a daughter, Mary. Henry's displeasure with Katharine was deepened by her father's disloyalty, culminating in Ferdinand's truce with France at a time when Henry's military victories over that country gave him the possibility of a decisive dominance. Katharine resisted Henry's attempts to annul the marriage or force her to withdraw to a nunnery. She insisted that only the pope could declare the marriage invalid.

Although the pope refused to invalidate the marriage, a papal legate was sent to England with authorization to try the issue jointly with Cardinal Wolsey. The legatine court was convened in May 1529 and Katharine appeared only to protest its jurisdiction. When it met again in June, the king stated his position and Katharine appeared and pleaded to him directly. She insisted that only Rome could decide the case, but the court rejected her protest, and Katharine withdrew from the proceedings. This is the scene that Shakespeare staged in act 2, scene 4 of his play, *Henry VIII*. It is Shakespeare's representation, with the great actress Sarah Siddons as Queen Katharine, that the painter George Harlow (1787–1819) has portrayed here. Henry sits in the center background and the two cardinals judging the case are in red. Harlow, a pupil of Sir Thomas Lawrence, specialized in historical scenes, of which this painting is considered his best. The work was completed around 1817, only two years before the artist's death at the age of thirty-two.

Pope Clement VII, after long vacillation, held the marriage valid and Henry broke with Rome and became head of the Church of England. Parliament passed the Act of Supremacy, repudiating the jurisdiction of the pope and the Roman church in England. Henry finally got his annulment from Katharine with the help of Thomas Cranmer, his own archbishop, and married Ann Boleyn, sacrificing Thomas More and many others in the process. Katharine died in 1536 and Elizabeth, Ann Boleyn's daughter, rather than Katharine's daughter, Mary, succeeded Henry.

The trial of Katharine's marriage settled nothing, but it has become a symbol of her demise as queen. Like *Joan of Arc*, (page 52) this painting also depicts the martyred heroine unsuccessfully pleading her cause before a tribunal of clergy prejudiced (i.e., pre-judged) against her. The momentous issues involved here shaped English law and history, the progress of the Reformation, church-state relations in England and throughout Europe, the concept of monarchy, and much more.

Both the playwright and the artist, seem to have subordinated the tensions of law, politics, and religion to those between the wronged wife and her frustrated husband. We see the development of law driven, or at least deeply influenced, by the actions of strong individuals in positions of power.

Colorplate 22. Oil on canvas. 31½×41" (80×104 cm). © From the Royal Shakespeare Company Collection, with the permission of the Governors of the Royal Shakespeare Theatre, Royal Shakespeare Theatre Picture Gallery, Stratford-upon-Avon.

Sir Thomas More

1530

Artist unknown

Thomas More (1477–1535), barrister, humanist, jurist, and martyr of the English Reformation, has become one of the heroes of the legal profession and, in 1935, four hundred years after his death, was made a saint of the Roman Catholic church. More was as complex a figure as Henry VIII, who, six years after making him lord chancellor of England, had him executed for treason.

For over ten years, Thomas More, son of a judge of the Court of King's Bench, was unable to decide on his choice of career. He considered following his father into the legal profession (he entered Lincoln's Inn in 1496 after an Oxford education, and became a barrister in 1501); accepting a religious vocation (a prospect that was ended by his marriage in 1505); or pursuing a life of study and contemplation like his friend, the great humanist, Erasmus of Rotterdam. Although finally deciding on the law, More maintained his strong interests in religion and scholarship. They undoubtedly shaped his views of law and of the proper role of judges, and probably contributed to his demise.

After ten years at the bar, More entered public service, becoming an under-sheriff in 1510 and a member of the King's Council in 1517. In 1516, he published *Utopia*, an important work of political philosophy that established him as one of the foremost intellects in England and abroad. In 1529, More succeeded Thomas Wolsey as lord chancellor, becoming the first layman to hold that post after three successive archbishops. He assumed the office with a strong sense of what a judge should be and with a firm reputation, like King Henry's, of enmity toward Martin Luther and the Protestant movement.

More became chancellor at a time when Henry was trying to end his marriage to Katharine of Aragon, to remove England from the jurisdiction of the pope, and to establish himself as head of a separate Church of England. Paradoxically, More's opposition to all of these efforts was probably known to Henry when he appointed More as chancellor. More used the office to improve the efficiency of Chancery, to make some reforms (although not as many as the bar had hoped for), and to continue his harsh persecution of Protestant heretics. As Henry pressed his claims, however, More's position became untenable and he resigned as chancellor in 1532, hoping to resume a life of scholarship.

With the help of Thomas Cromwell (who obtained legislation for the separation of the English church from Rome and the supremacy of Henry as head of the Church) and Thomas Cranmer (who annulled Henry's marriage to Katharine), Henry achieved his aims and married Ann Boleyn. His hopes for a male heir were never fulfilled, however, despite his six marriages, and his daughter with Ann Boleyn, Elizabeth, succeeded him. When Parliament passed a series of laws, including one requiring all subjects to take an oath acknowledging the supremacy of the king over the pope, More refused to comply, was indicted for treason, and subsequently executed.

For both the bench and bar of the common law world, Thomas More has come to symbolize the integrity and independence of the judiciary, the lawyer as a figure of conscience and courage, and the vulnerability of the intellectual who puts himself into the service of kings. This study of Thomas More, painted around 1530 by an unknown artist, convincingly portrays his rugged independence.

Colorplate 23. Oil on canvas. 22⁹/₁₆ × 17⁵/₈" (57.3 × 44.8 cm). Harvard Law Art Collection, Cambridge.

Sr Thomas Moore *Kn.^t L.^D Chancellor of England* 1530.

THE HAGUE MAGISTRATES RECEIVING THE OFFICERS OF THE CIVIC GUARD

1618

Jan van Ravensteyn

This large group portrait, completed by Jan van Ravensteyn in 1618, reflects the wealth and luxury of Holland during the Twelve Years' Truce between Spain and Holland (1609–1621). During this period of peace abroad, the Dutch enjoyed great prosperity through their domination of commerce and shipping throughout Europe and overseas. Domestically, however, it was a time of considerable political and religious conflict.

A group of moderate Calvinists, the Arminians or Remonstrants, which included the lawyer-statesman John van Oldenbarnevelt and the great jurist and philosopher Hugo Grotius, favored autonomous states, religious tolerance, and the right of local and provincial bodies to determine the status of religion in their areas. The opposing group, strict Calvinists called Gomarists or Anti-Remonstrants, supported a more centralized governmental structure and believed that the function of the state was to serve and defend an official Church, to repress religious dissent and enforce the Church's discipline.

The military ruler of the time, Prince Maurice of Orange, had settled in The Hague in 1585. Although not much interested in religion personally, he backed the Anti-Remonstrants for political reasons and staged a *coup d'etat*, disarming the civil guard in 1618. He then ordered the arrest of Oldenbarnevelt, Grotius, and two other leaders, in part for their alleged republican views. After a long trial, Oldenbarnevelt was beheaded, Grotius and another leader were sentenced to imprisonment for life,[1] and one other committed suicide.

Prince Maurice probably would have pardoned Oldenbarnevelt if he had asked for mercy. However, since that would have implied guilt, Oldenbarnevelt refused and was martyred. The similarity of this case to those of Socrates, Joan of Arc, and Thomas More suggests that it is yet another example of religious tensions, exacerbated by political conflict, leading to a miscarriage of justice.

At about the same time, at a meeting of the National Synod of the Reformed Church, the Re-

monstrants were outnumbered and suffered defeat on the issue of provincial sovereignty. They were finally condemned as heretics and excluded from the Church. Despite the victory of the Counter-Remonstrants at the Synod, the power of Maurice and of the municipal magistrates subsequently waned. Some see van Ravensteyn's painting as an attempt to bolster their credibility. The work was well received by both the magistrates and the guardsmen. Its realism and power reflect the skill of the artist who was master of The Hague guild and a distinguished portrait painter.

1. While in prison, Grotius wrote his *Introduction to Dutch Jurisprudence*, one of the great Dutch law books of all time. After his escape to France in 1625, he published his seminal work on international law, *The Law of War and Peace*.

Colorplate 24. Oil on canvas. 68 × 196¹/₁₆" (173 × 498 cm). Collection Haags Gemeentemuseum, The Hague.

1847

Robert-Fleury (Joseph Nicolas Robert Fleury)

The case of Galileo Galilei (1564–1642), Italian astronomer, physicist, and mathematician, is another noteworthy instance of the suppression of unpopular or "dangerous" ideas in the name of religion or at the instigation of religious officials. Early in his career, Galileo became convinced of the Copernican theory of the universe, that the planets revolve around the sun, and that the sun, not the earth, is the center of the universe. Initially, he avoided publicizing his views for fear of ridicule. When he did publish and teach the new concept, the Church proceeded against him—first in 1616 and then again in 1633. On each occasion, with great reluctance, he recanted and avoided serious punishment.

Galileo, a recognized scientist who had published technical works on physics, taught mathematics, first at the University of Pisa and, from 1592, as professor at the University of Padua. He had achieved fame and support from some Church leaders as a result of his demonstrations of the recently invented telescope for astronomical study. As he began to announce findings that supported the Copernican theory, he attracted opposition and enmity from Aristotelian scholars, Dominican preachers, and some Jesuits. In 1615, as Galileo's views were provoking increasing controversy, he was warned informally by the sophisticated and influential Cardinal Bellarmin. A few months later, in February 1616, he was specifically ordered, by direction of Pope Paul V, not to "hold, teach, or defend" Copernican doctrine which by then had been labeled heretical. Galileo agreed to obey that prohibition and he received assurances of support in his work from Cardinal Bellarmin and the pope.

Soon, however, Galileo resumed his Copernican study and teachings, hoping that the 1616 decree would be rescinded by the new pope, Urban VIII, who was personally supportive of him. In January 1632, Galileo's great work, *Dialoge die due massimi sistemi del mondo . . . (Dialogue Concerning the Two Chief World Systems—Ptolemaic and Copernican)* was published, and his troubles began anew. The book was widely praised and the first edition sold out quickly. But attacks from Galileo's enemies in the Church accelerated. By the end of 1632, the sale of the book was prohibited and Galileo was ordered to Rome by the Inquisition. He was charged with violating the decree of 1616 by his book and by other writings and teachings. He defended himself largely by disavowing his Copernican views and alleging his good intentions. Hearings were held between April and June 1633, before the commissary-general of the Inquisition, during which Galileo denied remembering the 1616 injunction against him. At times he was threatened with torture, but that was never employed. Finally, on June 23, 1633, he partially admitted the charges and recanted and stated: "I abjure, curse, and detest the aforesaid errors and heresies and generally every other error, heresy, and sect whatsoever contrary to the Holy Church . . ."[1]

Galileo was condemned as "vehemently suspected of heresy" and sentenced to indefinite imprisonment. The sentence was commuted by the pope to house arrest, which remained in effect throughout his last eight years. Galileo lived in seclusion on his estate near Florence and pursued his telescopic studies until he became blind in 1637. He actively continued his scientific work and correspondence to his death, obviously still holding to the Copernican theory.

This large painting of Galileo's trial before the Inquisition is by Joseph Nicolas Robert Fleury (1797–1890). Robert-Fleury was a French artist, from a family of painters. He specialized in historical scenes and used the realistic style employed by other French painters of trial scenes.

1. Giorgio de Santillana, *The Crime of Galileo* (Chicago: Phoenix Books, University of Chicago Press, 1955), 312.

Colorplate 25. Oil on canvas. 77⅜×121¼" (196.5×308 cm). Louvre, Paris.

THE LAWYER'S OFFICE

1628

Pieter de Bloot

Genre painting, a diverse and varied art form which represents scenes from ordinary life, is a valuable source of information about occupations and professions, clothing, furnishings, tools, and manners as seen in the routine activities of daily life. Accurate representation of color, texture, scale, light, and relationships have been its defining elements.

Historically, because such paintings were not commissioned by the state, the church, or wealthy patrons, they exhibited a freedom of expression. In societies accustomed to flattering portraits of the wealthy and political elite, and to large renditions of classical and historical scenes, genre paintings were often viewed as coarse, undignified, or even subversive. However, because such pictures seemed optimistic in their affirmation of human existence, and were tolerant, familiar, and often witty, they were very popular.

Genre painting was a popular art form in western Europe, reaching particular heights of quality and popularity in seventeenth-century Holland, when that country was enjoying economic leadership in Europe. Since lawyers were an integral part of Dutch life and society, it is not surprising that they and their work were often represented in genre painting. *The Lawyer's Office*, painted by Pieter de Bloot (1601–1658) in 1628 is a fine example. De Bloot was a versatile artist in Rotterdam who painted both landscapes and interiors.

The painting provides valuable detail for both the social historian and the legal historian. The size of the office, the diversity of classes among its clientele, and the varied costumes of both the clients and the figures behind the three desks are all noteworthy features. It appears to be an open office, with a "walk-in" business, presenting a variety of matters to the professionals who seem to perform several different functions.

The hanging of documents on the walls (which appears also in other Dutch paintings of lawyers), the books on the shelves, the attitude and posture of the figures, and the general sense of disarray and informality, add to the painting's documentary character. The sign on the side of the lawyer's desk is an old Dutch proverb discouraging litigation. It can be translated loosely as follows: "He who sues for a cow, may have to provide another cow." The statement still appears

in the offices of Dutch lawyers today.

De Bloot seems to typify here the essential qualities of Dutch genre painting in this period, namely an objective affection for the routine and ordinary; an attitude of familiarity (at times of intimacy) with the surroundings; and a sense of simplicity and frankness.

Colorplate 26. Oil on panel. 22⅜×32⅝″ (57×83 cm). Rijksmuseum, Amsterdam.

1655

Adriaen van Ostade

Adriaen van Ostade (1610–1685) of Haarlem is generally considered to be the most important and prolific of the seventeenth-century Dutch genre painters. Ostade, who trained in the studio of Franz Hals, specialized in scenes of peasant life and was sometimes called the Peasant Rembrandt. *The Village Lawyer*, painted in 1655, shows a very different scene from that portrayed by de Bloot in *The Lawyer's Office* (page 64). It is one of several by Ostade of lawyers at work and presents many of the qualities associated with genre painting. It is, however, simpler in composition than de Bloot's busy canvas, and more clearly portrays the individual features of its three figures, as compared to the unfinished faces in de Bloot's work.

This rural lawyer, practicing in what appears to be a tavern, lacks the special trappings and support staff in the large office shown by de Bloot. Ostade's lawyer has a more direct relationship with his clients and his dress is like theirs, although he wears the skull cap which was common among Dutch lawyers of the time.[1] We can probably assume that the village lawyer's practice was not much different from that of a country lawyer in other countries, including America, from the seventeenth through the nineteenth century. Land transactions and disputes, sales of livestock, damage claims, debt collection, and the drafting of legal documents such as wills, deeds, mortgages, and contracts, undoubtedly constituted the bulk of his work.

The law of the Netherlands as a whole was confused and uneven throughout the seventeenth century. It was a time of internal turmoil, religious and political conflict, and intermittent war. The movement for codification of provincial and municipal customary law in the previous century had given somewhat more coherence and reliability to the administration of justice, but the legal system was still very fragmented and decentralized, and legislation was inconsistent among the provinces. Despite the development and study of Roman law in the Dutch universities (whose scholars had studied in the major Italian centers of learning), Roman law had achieved relatively little authority in most of Holland. While great jurists like Hugo Grotius were influential abroad —the Dutch often set policy for international trade and commerce—the village lawyer practiced an older and less sophisticated form of customary law, with great variation from place to place.

Among the law books in the Netherlands at that time, a Dutch version of the *Sachsenspiegel* (page 34), called *Hollandscher sachsenspiegel* was more likely to be used by the village lawyer than the scholarly *Introduction to Dutch Jurisprudence*,[2] written by Grotius during his imprisonment (page 60) and first published in 1631. By the second half of the seventeenth century, however, when this painting was done, the Roman-Dutch law which Grotius had helped develop, was beginning to flourish through most of the country.

1. W. N. Hargreaves-Mawdsley, *A History of Legal Dress in Europe Until the End of the Eighteenth Century* (Oxford: The Clarendon Press, 1963), 113.

2. Hugo Grotius, *The Jurisprudence of Holland*, 2 vols. (Oxford: Clarendon Press, 1926, 1936).

Colorplate 27. Oil on panel. 14⅝ × 11¾" (37 × 30 cm). Allentown Art Museum, Allentown, Pennsylvania. Samuel Kress Memorial Collection. 1961.

LOUIS XIV PRESIDING AT THE COUNCIL OF THE PARTIES

Seventeenth century

Artist unknown

The long reign of Louis XIV (1638–1715) as king of France has become a symbol of absolute monarchy. When his father, Louis XIII, died in 1643, Louis succeeded to the throne although he was not yet five years old. After a revolt by the nobility and the *Parliament* of Paris in 1648, during which young Louis suffered hardship and indignity, the victorious Prime Minister Cardinal Mazarin reconstructed the government. Mazarin also taught Louis statecraft and other attributes of kingship. Upon the death of Mazarin in 1661, Louis announced that he would rule personally, directly, absolutely, and initially without a prime minister. He considered himself to be God's representative on earth—a ruler by divine right—and asserted that right with vigor for the rest of his life.

The history of French law under the Sun King was a mixture of achievement and reform along with tyranny and scandal. The judicial structures and procedures were subject to the concept of *justice retenue*, i.e., justice retained in the person of the king. The king was the final judge of disputes between his subjects and the ultimate law giver. Rather than a separation of powers, France had all power united in the king—*Rex animat lex*, 'the king gives life to the law.'

The chancellor was the king's highest officer in the administration of justice. He was appointed for life, could preside over any royal court, recommended judges for appointment, and worked through a multifaceted tribunal, the *conseil d'etat, privé, des parties, finances, et directions*. This council, operating separately under the various components of its full name, carried out different legal functions. Under the title of *conseil des parties*, it functioned as a high court, hearing appeals from lower court decisions, moving cases from one court to another, and nullifying decisions of lower courts or even of the *parliaments*. The chancellor presided over the council but there was always an empty chair opposite the chancellor, representing the symbolic presence of the king who could always preside if he chose to do so. On important occasions, Louis XIV did preside over the council, as shown in this painting by an unknown artist.

The bureaucracy of the chancellor in the administration of his many duties was large and varied, and included two hundred lawyers who represented the king and his government in preparing briefs for the high court of the *conseil*. They were called *avocat du roi* and were like Queen's Counsel in modern Britain.

Louis was anxious to make major legal reforms to correct past abuses. He wanted to simplify the legal system which then employed over seventy thousand men, and to unify both the law itself, through a single body of ordinances, and the agencies of justice. Louis saw himself as a new Justinian. He promulgated the Civil Ordinance of 1667, which reformed civil procedure and made it uniform throughout the kingdom, and the Criminal Ordinance of 1670, which did somewhat the same for criminal law and procedure. However, efficiency rather than justice was the major object of these reforms. Those accused of crimes in most instances still had no right of counsel; torture was permitted when a capital crime was suspected; and both the judges and the king were able to manipulate the new procedures for their own purposes.

Perhaps it is not surprising that the young king, who early in his reign had reminded the Parlement of Paris that he was the state *(L'etat, c'est moi!)*, should have in practice considered himself above the law. Despite some improvements in the legal system, he left a legacy of injustice, arbitrary rule, and corruption. Those conditions, continuing under his successors, were undoubtedly among the factors which led to the French Revolution.

Colorplate 28. Oil on canvas. 43⁵/₁₆ × 50⁷/₁₆". (110 × 129 cm). Versaille, Paris. Giraudon/Art Resource, NY.

THE SEAT OF JUSTICE IN THE PARLIAMENT OF PARIS

1723

Nicolas Lancret

The impact of King Louis XV (1710–1774) on French law and the legal profession was less marked than that of his predecessor, Louis XIV (page 68), although the reign of Louis XV was also quite long (1715 to 1774). He too became king when he was only five and was subordinated first to a regent (for eight years) and then to strong prime ministers for another twenty-one years.

It was not until 1744, after the death of Cardinal Fleury, prime minister since 1726, that Louis announced he would rule directly, without a prime minister. However, he lacked the will and strength to govern firmly, and gradually left the affairs of state to contentious ministers and court officials. He devoted much of his time and energy to a series of mistresses who often asserted themselves in political matters. Madame de Pompadour, his official mistress from 1745 to 1764, was particularly influential and often damagingly so.

Toward the end of Louis' reign, a major conflict developed with the *parliaments* that had significant legal effect. The *parliaments'* veto power over royal legislation had been suspended by Louis XIV, but was restored during the regency in Louis XV's reign. The magistrates of *parliament*, opposed to the king's policies with regard to religion and taxation, used this power to strengthen their position vis-à-vis the king. This new assertiveness, augmented by a union of the many provincial parliaments with the Parliament of Paris, enabled the magistrates to thwart the king in several important conflicts.

Finally, in 1771, Chancellor Maupeau ended the revolt of the magistrates and instituted a series of law reforms. These included restricting the Parliament of Paris to its judicial role; abolishing the sale of judgeships; placing the selection, appointment, and remuneration of judges in the control of the king; and prohibiting many practices which had led to the corruption of the judiciary. The administration of justice was vastly improved and justice was made more accessible, faster, and less expensive. Although the new system functioned well, it did not improve the king's popular image. The abandonment of these reforms under Louis XVI added to the pressures for Revolution.

This painting, *The Seat of Justice in the Parliament of Paris* (1723), by Nicholas Lancret (1690–1743) shows the young King Louis XV in the Grand Chamber of the parliament. It depicts Louis before the magistrates. It is the state occasion in 1723 on which Louis assumed the age of legal majority (thirteen), marking the end of the regency. Louis appears on a throne in the far corner of the hall (to the right of center), wearing mourning clothes for the recent death of his governess.

The occasion was called a *lit de justice* (bed of justice) since it involved registering the king's majority. Another *lit de justice* had been held in 1715 to mark the beginning of the regency. These grand scenes of royal spectacles were popular subjects for the artists of that time. In the historic conflicts between the king and parliament, the Parliament of Paris would on occasion refuse to register royal decrees, claiming that unregistered decrees had no legal effect. In response, the king would hold a *lit de justice* by which he would exercise his power to make law directly by decree and order its registering. The designation of this ceremony by that name may relate to the registry aspect of recognizing the king's majority in law.

Lancret was a student of Antoine Watteau and was a popular painter of genre scenes and large ceremonial or historical events. He was prolific and often received royal commissions for both paintings and palace decoration. This painting, undoubtedly done to attract royal patronage, remained with the artist, however, until his death and was ultimately sold by his widow. Louis XV did order six other paintings from Lancret who also worked on the decorations at Fountainebleau, Versailles, and other royal halls.

Colorplate 29. Oil on canvas. 22 × 32" (56 × 81.3 cm). Louvre, Paris. Scala/Art Resource, NY.

1789

Jacques-Louis David

The swearing of the *tennis court oath* by the deputies of the Third Estate[1] on June 20, 1789, was one of the crucial events of defiance to the king that preceded the French Revolution. When the deputies of the nonprivileged classes realized that they would be outvoted by the clergy and the nobility in the *Estates-General*, the traditional assembly, they formed a National Assembly. Louis XVI, hearing that many of the clergy were going to join with the Third Estate, ordered their usual meeting hall closed for repairs, purportedly in preparation for a forthcoming royal session to be held there. Finding the doors barred by soldiers, the delegates, on the motion of Dr. Guillotin (later known for inventing the Revolution's instrument of execution), moved to the nearby royal tennis court, where they swore an historic oath, which stated in part:

> "The National Assembly, considering that it has been summoned to establish a constitution of the kingdom, to effect a regeneration of public order, and to maintain the true principles of monarchy; that nothing can prevent it from continuing its deliberations in whatever place it may be forced to establish itself; and, finally, that wheresoever its members are assembled, *there* is the National Assembly;
>
> . . .[A]ll members of the Assembly shall immediately take a solemn oath not to separate . . . until the constitution of the realm is established and consolidated upon firm foundations . . ."[2]

The oath was taken orally first, as shown in this dramatic painting of 1791 by Jacques-Louis David, leading artist of the Revolution. Then all but one of the 577 deputies present at the tennis court signed the document. As shown by David, crowds of excited onlookers witnessed the event.

One week later, King Louis XVI relented and directed the clergy and nobility to join the Third Estate in order to write a constitution for France. The act of defiance represented by the oath, however, stirred emotions and encouraged those who sought more radical remedies.

The painting portrays many of the leading figures of the Revolution and others from more

moderate quarters of the opposition. The gesture of the extended right arm, used by David in his earlier revolutionary painting, *The Oath of the Horatii* (1785), now becomes a symbol of the movement's defiance. The three clergymen shown in the center foreground depict the role of the clergy in the meeting. However, one of those shown was actually not there and two later became enemies of the Revolution. Ironically, many of the patriots shown in fervid support were later consumed by the Revolution on the guillotine.

David later served on the Committee for General Security and signed arrest warrants himself. Finally, he too was imprisoned, but survived and subsequently became court painter to Napoleon.

1. The Third Estate consisted of the nonprivileged classes, (i.e., neither clergy nor nobility) before the French Revolution.

2. John Paxton, *Companion to the French Revolution* (Facts on File Publications, 1988), 185.

Colorplate 30. Oil on canvas. 25 $^9/_{16}$ × 35$^1/_8$" (65 × 89 cm). Musée Carnavalet, Paris. Bridgeman/Art Resource, NY.

MARRIAGE A LA MODE: THE MARRIAGE CONTRACT

1743

William Hogarth

Throughout history, law and lawyers have been frequent targets of popular anger and ridicule. By parody, satire, and even farce, artists and writers have focused on the pomposity, hypocrisy, and greed all too often apparent in the legal profession. England in the eighteenth century was rich with satirists of great literary and artistic skill. While Jonathan Swift was perhaps the major literary satirist, William Hogarth (1697–1764) was undoubtedly the leading graphic satirist of his time, both as an engraver and a painter. He often aimed his barbs at lawyers and the institutions of law, either illustrating the texts of others (as with his 1726 pictures for Samuel Butler's *Hudibras*) or in original series of his own (such as *The Harlot's Progress* and *The Rake's Progress*).

The series of six narrative paintings called *Marriage à la Mode* (1745) was perhaps his finest satirical work. Although the nobility and the wealthy landowners were the major objects of his attack, his sharp humor hit others, including lawyers, and such legal aspects of marriage as the nuptial contract and the dowry. The phrase, *marriage à la mode*, referred to a marriage arranged for the mutual advantage of the parents. The picture shown here, *The Marriage Contract*, was the first plate in this series and depicts the arrangements for the impending marriage of the son of the earl, Lord Squanderfield, (most names are, of course, descriptive of the characters who bear them) to the daughter of a wealthy merchant. The characters are, from left to right: the prospective bridegroom, son of the earl; the prospective bride, daughter of the merchant; Silvertongue, the lawyer; the merchant, holding the document of the marriage settlement; the moneylender, handing the earl his mortgage, now paid for with the merchant's money; another lawyer with "A Plan of a New Building..." (presumably being financed by the marriage); and finally, the earl, Lord Squanderfield.

In addition to the characters themselves, the six paintings are rich in symbolism and in contemporary references which would be clear to their intended audience. For example, the earl points to the chart of his family tree, which goes back to William the Conqueror. Most branches on the family tree are marked by coronets, symbols of nobility, but one branch which is broken off probably indicates a marriage to someone of humble or obscure origin.[1]

In works such as *Marriage à la Mode*, Hogarth painted as a pictorial dramatist. He himself wrote: "My picture is my stage, and men and women my players." While his engravings were very popular during his lifetime, his paintings did not sell well. He was shut out by the major art dealers who controlled the market, and his pictures did not attract buyers from among those who could afford paintings because these potential buyers were often the obvious subjects of his ridicule. With works such as these, however, Hogarth has provided a brilliant and witty view of the contradictions and the seamy sides of English life and English law in the eighteenth century.

1. The foregoing description of the content of the painting is based on notes on the series in *Hogarth's Graphic Works . . .*, compiled and with a commentary by Ronald Paulson (Yale University Press, 1965)1:267–275.

Colorplate 31. Oil on canvas. 27×35" (68.5×88.9 cm). The National Gallery, London.

1855

Tompkins Harrison Matteson

The persecution of individuals, usually women, who were accused of witchcraft, has constituted one of the more shameful chapters in legal history. Belief in witchcraft and the fear of witches goes back to ancient times in both Greece and Rome. European witch-hunts were often linked to the persecution of heretics and other dissidents, as in the case of Joan of Arc (page 52).

The most noteworthy American witch-hunt took place in the small Massachusetts town of Salem in 1692, although accusations and even executions had occurred earlier in Boston and elsewhere in the colonies. A group of girls and young women started a mass hysteria by initially accusing three women of witchcraft. The trials began in June 1692, under an English law of 1603 which prescribed the death penalty for witchcraft.

One of the twenty-six who were ultimately executed was George Jacobs, Sr., a patriarch of the community in his seventies, who had lived in Salem for thirty-three years, and owned a large amount of land. Jacobs is alleged to have said: "You tax me for a wizard, you may as well tax me for a buzzard. I have done no wrong." On August 19, 1692, Jacobs was hanged and his property seized by the sheriff.

The furor gradually subsided, and the accusers lost credibility, particularly when they sought to charge the wife of the governor and several other distinguished individuals. On October 29, 1692, the special court was dissolved and those prisoners who were tried upon the controversial "spectral" evidence were released. The subsequent trials resulted in acquittals. The procedures and the use of spectral evidence were declared unlawful.

This painting of the *Trial of George Jacobs* was completed by Tompkins Harrison Matteson (1813–1884) in 1855. Matteson was a painter of genre and historical scenes in upstate New York, where he was also active in politics and community service. This is a rather fanciful depiction of the trial. The building in which the trial is portrayed is certainly grander than any Salem structure of that time and this representation is more melodramatic than was likely. Jacobs appears at the right on one knee, with a red cape.

Colorplate 32. Oil on canvas. 39 × 53" (99 × 134.6 cm). Essex Institute, Salem.

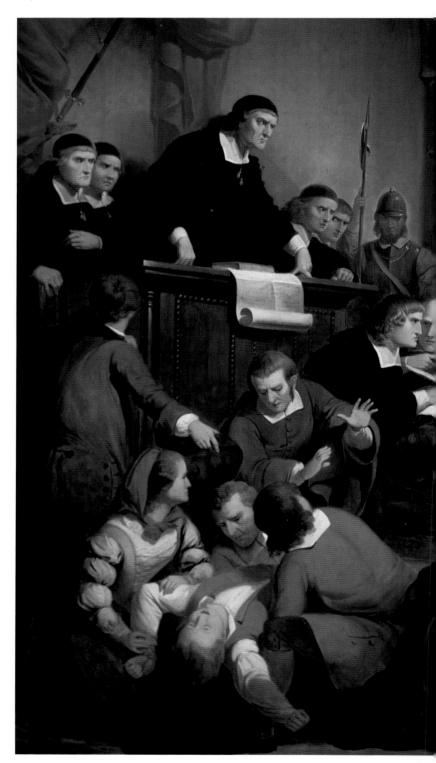

Patrick Henry Arguing the *Parson's Cause*

ca. 1830

George Cooke

Skill in rhetoric and oratory were as important for a lawyer in colonial America as in ancient Rome. It is not surprising that these were qualities possessed by a number of the early American patriots, since the arts of persuasion are valuable for any political leader, particularly in revolutionary times.

Patrick Henry (1736–1799), Virginia lawyer, was one of the most talented advocates of his time, an attribute which propelled him into the leadership of the colonial cause, first in Virginia and then throughout the colonies. He is best remembered for two radical speeches favoring separation from Britain. The first in the Virginia House of Burgesses on May 1765 against the Stamp Act which ended: "Caesar had his Brutus —Charles the first, his Cromwell—and George the Third may profit by their example." The other was his speech to the Virginia assembly on March 20, 1775, which included the words: "Give me liberty, or give me death."

One of Henry's greatest forensic triumphs, however, occurred early in his law practice, in his appearance on behalf of the Virginia colonists against their clergy, in a case known as the *Parson's Cause*. There were frequent disputes between the clergy and the tobacco planters arising from the Virginia tradition of paying the clergy in tobacco, a commodity whose value fluctuated widely. When tobacco was scarce and the price was high, the Virginia assembly enacted laws that allowed creditors to be paid at the rate of twopence a pound of tobacco, considerably below its then current value. The clergy successfully challenged the constitutionality of the Two-Penny Acts of 1755 and 1758 in England, arguing that the legislature could not legally authorize payment in money rather than tobacco when the crop was poor. Since such price-fixing was a long-established custom in Virginia, the complaint raised issues of self-government and aroused colonial animosity against both the clergy and the Crown. In a suit brought by a clergyman in Virginia, the county court, in November 1763, declared the law void. Patrick Henry was retained to argue for the local legislature before a jury on the amount of damages to be awarded.

His argument, pictured in this rather primitive painting by George Cooke, was not based on the legal issues involved in fixing damages. Instead, it focused on the greed of the clergy in seeking payment for religious duties; on their unwillingness to follow local law and tradition; and on the Crown's interference with the rights of free Virginians by annulling the acts. He painted the clergy and the king as enemies of the people by virtue of their selfishness, their lack of concern for the distressed colonists, and for ignoring the reciprocal obligations of church and state. The clergy, sensing Henry's oratorical effectiveness, left the courthouse before the verdict, threatening to charge him with treason. The jury awarded damages of one penny and Patrick Henry's reputation grew throughout Virginia. The case may have contributed to the inclusion in the Declaration of Independence of the grievance that the king had "refused his assent to laws, the most wholesome and necessary for the public good."

George Cooke (1793–1849), who probably completed this work by 1833, was a portrait painter, who occasionally did genre and historical paintings. He was born in Maryland and failed in several businesses before beginning to paint professionally in 1819. Cooke studied in France and Italy between 1826 and 1831. He was a protegé of the better-known painter, Daniel Pratt, who built a gallery to display Cooke's paintings in Prattville, Alabama, where Cooke was buried.

Colorplate 33. Oil on canvas. 28×36" (71.1×91.4 cm). The Virginia Historical Society, Richmond.

WASHINGTON ADDRESSING THE CONSTITUTIONAL CONVENTION

1856

Junius Brutus Stearns

Historical or patriotic scenes have long been popular subjects for officially commissioned paintings. Such paintings include murals or large canvases often intended for display in public buildings. Although many of these paintings were undistinguished and sometimes even of poor quality, others reflected the creativity of great artists stimulated by events about which they cared deeply. Some of the paintings by Jacques-Louis David of events of the French Revolution (page 72) have that distinction.

The important events of the American Revolution and America's independence have frequently been painted for public display. These include scenes from the life of George Washington, the signing of the Declaration of Independence, the major battles and dramatic episodes in the Revolutionary War, and the Federal Constitutional Convention.

The Constitutional Convention took place in Philadelphia during the hot, humid summer of 1787. In three months of drafting and debate, the delegates hammered out a document that was to govern the newly independent republic and establish the relationships between the federal government and the often contentious states that had created it. It turned out to be one of the major contributions of American political experience, and undoubtedly added a great measure of stability to the new nation and its government.

George Washington had not wanted to attend the convention, but since everyone agreed that his unifying presence was essential for the success of the proceedings, he finally agreed to attend and to preside. Despite his important role in holding the group together, he often sat with the Virginia delegation while others presided, and spoke formally only twice. The first time he spoke was to accept the presidency of the convention. And then, in the closing minutes of the last day of the convention, September 17, 1787, just as the delegates were about to sign the document, one of them moved that the ratio of representation in the House of Representatives be changed. Washington then gave his only substantive address, in support of the resolution. The change

passed unanimously, and the signing then took place, completing the work of the convention.

There have been many paintings of the convention, most of them now hanging in legislative halls, historical societies, and museums.[1] This one, by Stearns, is one of the most frequently reproduced.

Junius Brutus Stearns (1810–1885) was a portrait, genre, and historical painter. He is perhaps best known for his series on the life of Washington, including *Washington Addressing the Constitutional Convention*.

1. Several are described by Michael Kammen in *A Machine That Would Go Of Itself: The Constitution in American Culture* (New York: Alfred A. Knopf, 1986), 405–406.

Colorplate 34. Oil on canvas. 37½ × 54" (95.3 × 137.2 cm). Virginia Museum of Fine Arts, Richmond. Gift of Colonel and Mrs. Edgar W. Garbisch.

1833

J. B. Mauzaisse

Artistic commemorations of patriotic and historical events often have a tendency toward kitsch. This illustration of the durability of the Napoleonic code, by the relatively minor French painter of religious and historical subjects, Jean Baptiste Mauzaisse (1784–1844), certainly possesses that dubious quality. Nevertheless, the painting reflects the justifiable pride of the French nation in one of the great landmarks of modern legal history and the important role that Napoleon played in influencing that legislation. The codes[1] developed by French lawyers under Napoleon Bonaparte, particularly the Civil Code of 1804, have influenced the development of the civil law system throughout the world. These codes, having undergone relatively few changes, remain the bedrock of civil law in every one of the many countries living under that system.

The ancient codes of the Semitic peoples, the customary codes of early Europe, and most American codes merely collected existing law without changing it substantially. The French codes promulgated under Napoleon, however, comprehensively rewrote and reorganized the law. While based on Roman law and concepts they provided a form of law which was technically and substantively new. Although consisting of general legal propositions, the codes could be applied by deduction and analogy to specific cases. Jean Etienne Marie Portalis (1746–1807), the chief drafter of the Civil Code, described the theory as follows:

"The task of legislation is to determine the general maxims of law, taking a large view of the matter. It must establish principles rich in implications rather than descend into the details of every question that might possibly arise."[2]

The historian, Philippe Sagnac (1868–1954) characterized the accessible style in these terms:

"The Civil Code should be simple and clear, like the laws of nature. It must be reduced to a small number of articles that flow logically from general principles of the new democratic society. The individual will know the subtleties and infinite complications that chicanery invents at his expense."[3]

The Napoleonic codification successfully achieved a number of goals. The law was to be accessible to all; uniform throughout France; and based on democratic principles and economic liberalism. This involved sweeping changes in French law and gradually affected all aspects of French life. The Civil Code rested on three fundamental principles: private property, freedom of contract, and family solidarity.

The drafters also sought to secularize French society and reduce the role of the Catholic church in domestic relations and family law. To that end, the code treated marriage as a civil contract and redefined the grounds for nullifying a marriage. Earlier attempts at a national code during the Revolution failed, but Napoleon, the autocrat, was able to resolve conflicting interests and force the compromises necessary for consensus.

The code is still considered a masterpiece of French prose, and has been called the greatest book of French literature by the poet Paul Valéry. The Civil Code was supposed to have been read regularly by the novelist Stendahl, as a stylistic model for his own writing. It was quickly translated into many languages and its popularity spread throughout Europe. Similar codes were enacted in most of the countries of the world which were not under the common law system. What had started as a French achievement became a model for a worldwide legal revolution.

1. *Code Civil* (1804); *Code de Procédure Civile* (1806); *Code de Commerce* (1807); *Code Pénal* (1810); and *Code d'Instruction Criminelle* (1811). These are considered the *Napoleonic codes*; there are, however, other minor codes in French law which reflect the same principles and style.

2. Herman, Combe, Carbonneau, *The Louisiana Civil Code: A Humanistic Appraisal* (New Orleans: Tulane Law School, 1981), 16.

3. Ibid., 13.

Colorplate 35. Oil on canvas. 51½ × 63" (131 × 160 cm). Le Musée National de Château de Malmaison, Rueil, France. Giraudon/Art Resource, NY.

1820

Thomas Rowlandson

nglish caricaturists and satirists found a rich field for their humor and scorn in the law and its often pompous officials. This was particularly true in the Golden Age of English caricature, from the middle of the eighteenth century to the 1820s. We have already seen an example of William Hogarth's work in this field (page 74). Another great practitioner of graphic satire was Thomas Rowlandson (1756–1827), a London artist. Rowlandson, a superb draftsman, made many prints, but did some of his finest work in watercolor. Although initially a portrait and landscape painter, largely in oil, his drawings and watercolors gradually attracted the attention and praise of contemporary leading artists.

When a wealthy aunt died in Paris leaving Rowlandson a large inheritance and the means of independence, his free spirit was released. Gambling, bad investments, and pleasure-seeking, however, dissipated the inheritance. He then married, settled down, and began to produce illustrations for Rudolph Ackermann, a new publisher and color printer. The contractual arrangement was successful and Rowlandson did much work for Ackermann. But frequently, whenever he had funds, Rowlandson would take to the road, mixing work with adventure and carousing. His total body of work provided an incredibly rich and sweeping view of English life. Shown here are two biting examples of his social commentary—*Marshalsea Prison* (1820) and *Reading the Will* (page 86).

The Marshalsea Prison was established in the fourteenth century across the Thames River from Westminster and the City of London in the borough of Southwark. Initially it served as the prison for the Marshalsea Court (held by the Marshal of the Royal household), hence its name. It was primarily used to confine debtors and those in contempt of the king, until 1842 when it was closed. Throughout the centuries, it had a continuing reputation for cruelty and poor conditions, but varying degrees of comfort, relief from restrictions, and even privileges (including removal of irons, food from outside, family visits, and prostitutes) could be purchased from the warden. Fees were also charged on admission and discharge, even after a defendant's acquittal. These fees were finally prohibited by an Act in 1815. Despite the

prison reforms of the eighteenth century, poor conditions persisted in most English prisons. Prisoners wandered freely within the prison; debtors could, for the usual fee, have their family with them and even engage in a trade.

Rowlandson shows here the corpulent and rather nasty-looking jailer or warden admitting what appears to be a group of new prisoners. The prison looks crowded and disorganized; the prisoners idle, disreputable, and carousing rather than mistreated. Perhaps Rowlandson was particularly sensitive to the plight of debtors since his father had been bankrupt when the artist was a boy and, as a result, young Thomas had been sent to live with an uncle.

Colorplate 36. Watercolor on paper. 5¾ × 9¼" (14.6 × 23.5 cm). Boston Public Library, Boston.

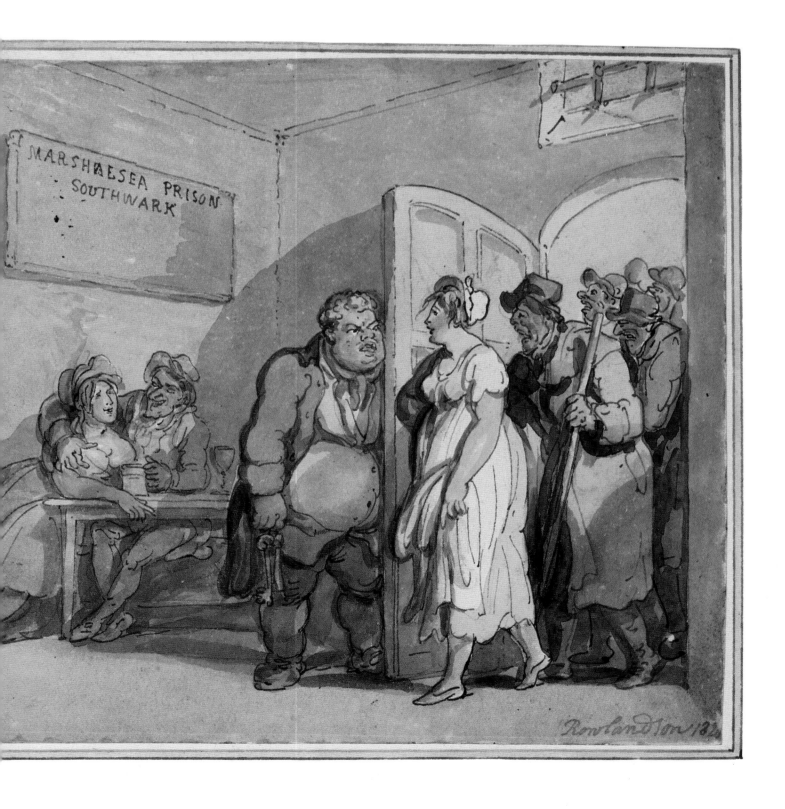

Early nineteenth century

Thomas Rowlandson

A bequest in a will was frequently used as a literary device in English novels to move the plot or change its direction, to present a central character with an opportunity or a disappointment, or simply to inject humor (or perhaps pathos) into the story. The reading of the will to the deceased's family and friends after the demise of the testator, usually by a solemn or pompous lawyer, was typically the focal event for this purpose. The drama of the occasion was heightened by the element of suspense and the emotional reactions of those present when they heard the good or bad news. Graphic artists also used this scene to expose human frailties.

Thomas Rowlandson depicted both the writing of a will and, in several drawings, the reading of a will. This watercolor, *Reading the Will*, is a fine example of his social satire and of his use of humor to illustrate the emotions revealed by the various individuals hearing the will. Moving generally from left to right, note the following characters: an outraged and disappointed heir (waving his stick), who is being consoled by a parson and supported by a youth, perhaps his son; the joyful beneficiary (waving his hat); the widow, looking perplexed; a lawyer reading the will over the coffin, surrounded by other relatives; an eavesdropper listening at the door; and a young woman who has fainted (cause unknown) with a friend or relative ministering to her.

The date of this drawing is undetermined, but it postdates the large inheritance which Rowlandson himself received on the death of his aunt in Paris. This benefactor, the widow of his Uncle Thomas, had also helped young Thomas earlier in his life. Before he was sixteen, she invited him to Paris and financed his art studies there. She gave him money regularly thereafter and encouraged his interest in a career in art. At her death, in 1789, she left him most of her estate, which he then lost through gambling and high living. Thus Rowlandson, from his own experience, was well aware of the blessings and dangers of sudden inherited wealth, and of the human comedy that it often provoked.

Colorplate 37. Watercolor on paper. 6 × 9¼" (15.2 × 23.5 cm). Boston Public Library, Boston.

TRIAL OF THE CAPTIVE SLAVES

ca. 1940

Hale Woodruff

Fifty-four Africans who comprised the slave cargo on the Spanish schooner, the *Amistad*, mutinied in 1839 in Cuban waters and took control of the vessel. The slaves killed most of the crew during their revolt and several of their own people died as well. The surviving slaves, under their leader, Cinque, then attempted to sail the ship back to Africa. Two Spanish crew members who were spared because of their navigational skills, however, directed the vessel north to United States waters, at first hoping to be intercepted by British cruisers. After sailing for two months, the *Amistad* was finally boarded in Long Island Sound by sailers from a United States naval ship, and towed into New London, Connecticut.

The slaves were imprisoned in New Haven for murder, mutiny, and piracy. Those charges were finally dropped after many legal complications. Conflicting claims for the vessel and the slaves, however, were then brought in the U.S. District Court by the Spanish slave-owners, the Americans who captured them, and others. Abolitionists seeking freedom for the slaves intervened and secured distinguished counsel for them, including John Quincy Adams and Roger Baldwin. The District Court ruled that the slaves "be delivered to the president of the United States to be transported to Africa . . ." and conducted home. That decision was appealed to the Supreme Court of the United States by the federal attorney general on the ground that a treaty with Spain required the slaves be returned to their owner. The Supreme Court, however, affirmed the lower court decision, but changed the disposition and ordered that the slaves be "declared to be free, and that they be dismissed from the custody of the Court . . ."[1] Unfortunately, funds were not available immediately to transport them home and they did not reach Africa until January 1842.

This painting, entitled *Trial of the Captive Slaves*, was one of a series of three murals on the case. The murals were painted by a distinguished

African American artist, Hale Woodruff (1900–1980), for the Savery Library of Talladega College in Talladega, Alabama. Woodruff, a prolific painter, printmaker, and muralist, studied in Paris and with Diego Rivera in Mexico. He taught art at Atlanta University (1931–1945) and at New York University (1945–1968).

Woodruff's dramatic portrayal of the trial in the United States District Court features Cinque, the leader of the mutiny, standing alone in front of the judge's bench and facing one of the Span-ish sailors who points to him in accusation. The cause was a focus of antislavery attention during its two years in the courts. Its relatively happy ending was unusual among the many cases that returned escaped or fugitive slaves to their owners.

1. Decision in *United States v. The Amistad*, 40 U.S. (15 Peters) 518 (1841).

Colorplate 38. Oil on canvas. 12⅛ × 40″ (30.8 × 101.6 cm). The New Haven Colony Historical Society. Gift of the Estate of George W. Crawford, 1973.

JOHN BROWN GOING TO HIS HANGING

1942

Horace Pippin

John Brown (1800–1859), radical abolitionist, became a hero and martyr of the militant antislavery movement by his unsuccessful raid on the federal arsenal at Harper's Ferry, Virginia (now West Virginia) in October 1859. The raid was part of Brown's quixotic plan to invade the South, liberate the slaves by force, and establish a new government. In May 1858, Brown had organized a convention in Canada, at which he and a small group of supporters drafted a "Provisional Constitution and Ordinances for the People of the United States," set up a government structure on paper, and established an army, with himself as commander-in-chief.

Brown led that small army of nineteen men, which included five blacks, in a futile night attack on the small town. The plot failed for want of support, and inexplicably the invaders did not escape when they could have done so. They were held in check by Maryland and Virginia troops, and then captured by United States Marines under the command of Colonel Robert E. Lee. Ten of the insurgents (including two of Brown's sons) and seven others were killed in the fighting. Ironically, the first person killed was a free black, the baggage-master at the railroad station, who was shot by one of Brown's men. Brown was wounded slightly and imprisoned. He was charged with treason and conspiracy to commit treason and murder, found guilty, and sentenced to death. He was hanged on December 2, 1859, having conducted himself with dignity throughout.

Brown believed himself to be an instrument in the hands of God to free the slaves. Despite the impossibility of the Harper's Ferry attack, it was the most forceful act yet taken against slavery, and aroused great public discussion of the issue. Brown had polarized the country. To some he was a martyr in a sacred cause; to others he was a murderer and a traitor to his race and his country. His militancy had sharply divided the country into proslavery and antislavery camps, pushing it inexorably closer to civil war.

Like the *Amistad* mutiny, John Brown's raid continued to reflect in the music, literature, and art of later generations the unfulfilled aspirations of African Americans. This painting, *John Brown Going to His Hanging* (1942) by the black primitivist, Horace Pippin, is an outstanding example of such representations. Pippin (1888–1946) was a self-taught folk artist, who was "discovered" by N. C. Wyeth, the famous illustrator, in 1937, and quickly achieved wide recognition.

Pippin had been severely wounded while serving in the front lines of combat in France during World War I. Still suffering from partial paralysis of his right arm, he taught himself to burn images on wood with a hot poker braced between his arm and his knee. He could then paint in the grooves made by the poker. In 1930, he began painting with oils directly on canvas. Pippin first envisioned his proposed picture in his mind and then gave it form and color on the canvas. The resultant images had great strength and brilliant color.

Like other African-American artists, Horace Pippin was interested in the life of John Brown as a subject for his work. Pippin's grandmother had told him of being present at Brown's hanging. Pippin did a series of three oil paintings: Brown reading his Bible; Brown on trial; and Brown being taken to his hanging. In the last one, shown here, although most of the spectators are facing John Brown, one elderly black woman turns her back on the proceedings in what appears to be either grief or anger, or perhaps both. That figure is said to represent Pippin's grandmother. Since all of the other figures in the picture seem to be white, the black woman may also represent African Americans in general.

Colorplate 39. Oil on canvas. 24⅛×30¼" (61.2×76.8 cm). The Pennsylvania Academy of the Fine Arts, Philadelphia. John Lambert Fund.

1842

Tompkins Harrison Matteson

Whether the frontier was just beyond the Appalachians, the Mississippi, or the Rockies, backwoods justice has always been a part of American folklore. As such, it has also been a frequent theme in American literature and painting. The associated images usually included one or two impassioned lawyers, a nervous defendant or two anxious parties, a skeptical judge, an attentive or puzzled jury, and a mixed audience of spectators, ranging from country bumpkins to shrewd horse-traders. The scene is typically set in distinctly nonjudicial surroundings—a tavern, a barn, or even outdoors.

Justice's Court in the Backwoods (1842), a genre painting by Tompkins Harrison Matteson (1813–1884)[1], is a typical example of such a scene. It shows two lawyers disputing a point of law with a thoughtful justice of the peace in what appears to be a country tavern. Most of the other elements described above are present.

The office of justice of the peace in America, still common in small towns and rural areas, derives from a medieval English model. The official was originally charged with keeping the peace and trying criminal cases and some civil suits. In colonial America, the justice of the peace and his court flourished as the lowest level of the judicial structure, and frequently had administrative duties as well. After Independence, both the criminal and civil jurisdiction in most states were gradually reduced—the former to misdemeanors and minor offenses, the latter to smaller claims and petty disputes. The office did not require legal training and most justices of the peace were (and still are) laypersons.

The pragmatic quality of the justice administered by these officers can be seen in the following charge to a jury by Judge John Dudley of New Hampshire, a trader and farmer by profession who, between 1785 and 1797, also served as associate justice of the Supreme Court of New Hampshire:

"Gentlemen, you have heard what has been said in this case by the lawyers, the rascals! ...The talk of law. Why, gentlemen, it is not law that we want, but justice! They would govern us by the common law of England. Common-sense is a much safer guide ...A clear head and an honest heart are worth more than all the law of the lawyers.

There was one good thing said at the bar. It was from Shakspeare [sic!],—an English player, I believe . . .It is our duty to do justice between the parties, not by any quirks of the law out of Coke or Blackstone,—books that I never read and never will."[2]

Matteson undoubtedly had personal experience with justices of the peace and their courts. He spent the first twenty years of his life in small towns in upstate New York where his father was a deputy sheriff. Matteson received his first art lessons from a Native American prisoner awaiting trial for murder. After ten productive years of painting in Manhattan, he returned upstate and settled in Shelburne, New York in 1850, where he spent the rest of his life.

1. *The Trial of George Jacobs*, page 76, is another example of Matteson's work. He is probably best known for the *Spirit of '76*, a patriotic painting of the American Revolution.

2. Anton-Hermann Chroust. *The Rise of the Legal Profession in America* (Norman University of Oklahoma Press, 1965), 2: 42–43.

Colorplate 40. Oil on canvas. 31³/₄×44" (80.6×112 cm). New York State Historical Association, Cooperstown.

Preliminary Trial of a Horse Thief: Scene in a Western Justice's Court

1877

John Mulvaney

Court proceedings on the Western frontier in the nineteenth century offered an even rougher form of justice than the backwoods of the East. The presumption of innocence, the rules of evidence, and other procedural safeguards were frequently overlooked. "Hanging judges" such as Roy Bean and Isaac Parker made a quick and arbitrary disposition of most cases reaching them. Law enforcement was erratic, police and peace officers were few and often corrupt, and lynchings were common. Because of their importance as the central means of transportation and their high cost, the stealing of a horse was a very serious —and sometimes a capital—crime. Convictions were routine, appeals virtually impossible, and punishment swift and at times brutal.

Preliminary Trial of a Horse Thief: Scene in a Western Justice's Court (1877), a chromolithograph by John Mulvaney, depicts a proceeding of this kind. The informality of the forum seems evident from the nature of the surroundings and the placement of the figures. The defendant appears to be the bearded man with the bandaged hand and brown greatcoat, standing next to the crate in the center of the picture. The sheriff is probably the individual holding handcuffs seated next to the defendant. The judge is certainly one of the three men seated at the table to the left. Note the lawbook on the floor under the table; that location may indicate the low status of formal legal concepts in these courts.

The crude justice of the old West has been a frequent subject of literature, the cinema, and popular culture generally. The general view has been negative, emphasizing its arbitrary and harsh features. Another, more tolerant description states:

> "But because the frontier courts and the frontier lawyers obviously shunned formality, decorum, and even a modest mastery of the law, it must not be inferred that the administration of justice in the pioneer communities was essentially a travesty or a farce. The judges and the lawyers, in the main, were men of homespun integrity and sterling common sense. In doing justice, the latter quality often had to supplement the law, which had not yet become adjusted to frontier conditions. The pioneers, on the whole, were thoughtful, earnest, and independent people who not only possessed a natural genius for self-government, but also recognized the necessity as well as the authority of law and order; and the courts, the judges, and the laws were established in the spirit of a rampaging frontier society."[1]

John Mulvaney (1844–1906) was a prominent painter of the American West, although his work ranges widely over many subjects, including portraits and political events. He was born in Ireland, migrated to this country at the age of twelve, and later studied art in Germany and Belgium. His most famous work was a carefully researched depiction of the battle between the Sioux Indians and the U.S. Army at Little Bighorn. It was a huge painting called *Custer's Last Rally* and was exhibited in several cities here and abroad. Mulvaney became an alcoholic in his later life and committed suicide by drowning in the East River, in New York City. *Preliminary Trial of a Horse Thief* was his first work of note and was exhibited at the National Academy of Design.

1. Anton-Hermann Chroust, *The Rise of the Legal Profession in America* (Norman: University of Oklahoma Press, 1965), 2:97–98, footnotes omitted.

Colorplate 41. Chromolithograph. 21⅛ × 28½" (53.7 × 72.4 cm). The Bancroft Library, University of California; Berkeley.

THREE LAWYERS

ca. 1843–1846

Honoré Daumier

Honoré-Victorin Daumier (1808–1879) is generally considered the finest French caricaturist of the nineteenth century (and perhaps of any century). The legal profession was one of the major targets of his satire. Daumier was a prolific and versatile artist. He was not only a masterful draftsman, specializing in lithography, but also a superb painter and an occasional sculptor. Although he generally avoided involvement in artistic circles, he was respected and praised by the leading artists and writers of his time. Balzac compared him to Michelangelo; Baudelaire to Moliere.

Between 1845 and 1848, thirty-nine of Daumier's lithographic caricatures of lawyers, judges, and clients, appeared in the weekly journal, *La Caricature*. They were later published as a series entitled *Lawyers and Justice*. In 1851, another series of four appeared in *Le Charivari* under the title, *Lawyers and Litigants*. But Daumier also pursued this subject in other media, particularly in watercolor and oil. The oil painting shown here, *Three Lawyers* in conversation, is one of the finest of his legal paintings.

Daumier's interest in law and his jaundiced view of the legal profession and the judiciary was in part a function of his political radicalism and his critical portrayal of French bourgeois society in general. It undoubtedly also stemmed from his many unhappy experiences with the law and its officers which began when Daumier, as a youth, accompanied his father, an artisan and a poet, to the Palais de Justice in the latter's futile efforts to straighten out his affairs. His father had wanted Honoré to become a lawyer or a notary. He, in fact, worked for a while as office boy to a bailiff, and then had several years of training with lawyers. He became an artist, however, learned lithography, and, with the 1830 revolution, turned to political satire. In 1831 he was tried and convicted, and was imprisoned in 1832 for six months for a satirical print portraying King Louis-Philippe as Gargantua. Daumier was never again indicted (even after he continued virulent attacks on the government and society), but he had other trou-

ble with the law. In 1841, for example, bailiffs seized his personal possessions for indebtedness and sold them at public auction.

Not surprisingly, lawyers first appear as objects of his satirical attack in 1832 shortly after his incarceration. The legal lithographs mix tragedy and comedy, but rarely depart from a very critical view of lawyers of all kinds. Judges are also ridiculed, but somewhat more gently than the lawyers. The difficult economic conditions in France that were one of the causes of the 1848 revolution were reflected both by Victor Hugo and Daumier in different ways. In *Les Miserables*, Hugo portrayed the insensitivity of the *judge* to the effects of poverty and starvation as causes of Valjean's crime. Daumier in his work of that time focused on the insensitivity of *lawyers* to the plight of their clients.

After 1848, Daumier concentrated on painting rather than lithography, but remained a social critic. He supported the revolution of 1848 and the Paris Commune of 1871. An authority on Daumier described the continuing significance of his satire of lawyers, as follows:

"More than a century later they have lost none of their vigor and power. Every time we take a fresh look at these plates and study them closely, we realize that Daumier was a powerful artist whose personages, silhouettes, expressions, and gestures of every kind leave a deep imprint on our minds...Paul Valery was well aware that 'with Daumier ridicule is a kind of rehearsal for the Last Judgement and all his caricatures give the impression of a moral or intellectual Dance of Death'. Thus in this series portraying the unworthy servants of Justice, satire has indeed passed judgement and has condemned them for posterity".[1]

1. Julien Cain, "Preface", in Daumier, *Lawyers and Justice* (Boston: Boston Book and Art, 1971), [21].

Colorplate 42. Oil on canvas. 16×13" (40.6×33 cm). © The Phillips Collection, Washington, D.C.

1891

Sir Leslie Ward ("Spy")

The English weekly magazine, *Vanity Fair*, which was published from 1868 to 1914, contained many of the finest caricatures of that period. More than half of the 2,500 published were from the pen of "Spy," the pseudonym of Sir Leslie Ward (1851–1922), a prolific caricaturist and artist.

Both of Ward's parents were painters and there were painters among his forebears on his mother's side for several generations. Under his pen name "Spy" he was one of the most popular of *Vanity Fair*'s artists for thirty-six years and was knighted in 1918. Ward's work was done in color and reproduced by lithography.

The caricatures turned what had been a marginal magazine into one of the most popular and influential journals in Britain and the English-speaking world generally. The demand for the individual caricatures was so great that they were reprinted and sold separately, and even today continue to be widely collected.

There were caricatures of politicians, lawyers, judges, physicians, clergy, sportspeople, literary figures, and the military—leaders from all segments of the establishment—each accompanied by a brief and sometimes biting biography of the subject, usually written by the founder and editor of *Vanity Fair*, Thomas Gibson Bowles (1842–1922). The first two cartoon portraits to appear in *Vanity Fair*, of Benjamin Disraeli and Disraeli's archrival William Gladstone, were by an Italian artist, Carlo Pelligrini (1839–1899), who set the style that influenced Leslie Ward and other *Vanity Fair* caricaturists.

Barristers, solicitors, and judges were popular subjects for Ward and for *Vanity Fair*. Sir Alexander Cockburn, lord chief justice of England, was the subject of the first legal caricature to appear in December 1869, drawn by Pelligrini, who used the pen name "Ape." The biographical sketches of legal figures accompanying the caricatures were among the most trenchant that Bowles wrote. The caricatures themselves remain popular decorations for lawyer's offices today.

The illustration shown here, *Bench and Bar*

(with the Earl of Malsbury), drawn by Leslie Ward, is unusual in that it is one of the few group portraits in *Vanity Fair*.[1] The *Bench and Bar* was accompanied in its original publication (December 5, 1891) by a satirical essay, signed "Jehu Junior."[2] *Vanity Fair* had been sold by Thomas Bowles in 1889, so it is unlikely to have been written by him. The essay begins in general terms, as follows:

"Of all the wares and merchandises that are sold in this *Vanity Fair*, there is none more rightly held in high esteem than Justice; which though it be a very costly article here, has yet been famous throughout all the world for many a century."

It then goes on to describe individuals depicted, noting that the scene is of the first day of Michaelmas Term in the Central Hall of the Royal Courts of Justice, near the Strand in London. The description of the judges concludes: "These are some of the Judges who are now dispensing Justice at exceeding cost and with most incredible delay, yet very skillfully, in this *Vanity Fair*." The lawyers are then treated, with a concluding comment of equal bite that states in part:

"These are specimens of those who fatten while their clients are ruined. They work well, and no fair as better specimens, nor more knowing in the law, which they make more complicated as they go: in recompense for which they have promoted a very beautiful system by which their clients are allowed no more access to them than is needed for the payment of their high fees..."

1. The identity of some of the individuals in the drawing is given in Rupert Collens, *25 Legal Luminaries from Vanity Fair* (London: Lambourn Publications, 1990), 6–7.

2. *Vanity Fair*, supplement, 5 Dec. 1891, 441–442.

Colorplate 43. Colortype. 13¾ × 19½" (35 × 49.5 cm) Harvard Law Art Collection, Cambridge.

A Class at the University of Pennsylvania Law School

1879

Mary Franklin

American legal education in the last quarter of the nineteenth century underwent changes in theory and pedagogy that would affect it for at least the next hundred years. The concept of law as a science which could be taught by the case study method had been introduced at the Harvard Law School by Christopher Columbus Langdell during his deanship from 1870 to 1895.[1] This approach spread quickly to a few other law schools (often having to overcome spirited resistance), and it gradually replaced the more vocationally oriented lecture system. By 1895, case study was used almost exclusively at Columbia, Harvard, Iowa, Northwestern, the University of Pennsylvania, and Stanford.[2] By the mid–twentieth century, it was the prevalent method of instruction in all accredited American law schools.

Although the University of Pennsylvania had a professorship in law since 1790, the Law School was not firmly established until 1852. The depiction of a class of the University of Pennsylvania Law School, painted by Mary Franklin (active 1876–1912) in 1879, shows that school in its last years of the old lecture method of study. It was then a two-year course of study, and graduation entitled one to bar admission without the requirement of a clerkship or bar examination. The 1878–97 catalog indicated that "Instruction is conveyed by lectures . . ." The school that year had 126 students (all men) and a faculty of five. Women were not admitted to the Law School until 1881, when Caroline B. Kilgore (who had already received an M.D. degree in 1864) became its first woman student. She was the first woman to become a physician in New York, and later became the first woman to practice before the Supreme Court of Pennsylvania.

Mary Franklin's painting shows Dr. E. Coppée Mitchell, dean of the Law School from 1872 to 1887, lecturing in what seems to be a rather informal setting. The painting was for some years incorrectly entitled *George Sharswood, Professor of Law, Lecturer at the Philadelphia Law School* Sharswood was, in fact, a founder of the Pennsylvania Law School and professor of law from 1850 to 1868, but when this picture was painted he was chief justice of the Supreme Court of Pennsylvania.

Franklin was born in Athens, Georgia, and studied at the Pennsylvania Academy of the Fine Arts under Thomas Eakins from 1876 to 1880. (She was a classmate and friend of Eakins' wife, Susan MacDowell Eakins.) This painting, which brought Franklin some distinction, was done during her study with Eakins, and shows Eakins' influence on her work. Franklin exhibited portraits, still lifes, and genre paintings at the Pennsylvania Academy from 1877 to 1896, and at the National Academy of Design from 1879 to 1881.[3] Little is known about her later life and career except that she studied and worked in France at times between 1901 and 1912. Based on this strong portrayal of the clubby atmosphere of the nineteenth century law school, Franklin seems to merit more interest than she has received.

1. Langdell stated his theory as follows: ". . .law, considered as a science, consists of certain principles or doctrines. To have such a mastery of these as to be able to apply them with constant facility and certainty to the ever-tangled skein of human affairs, is what constitutes a true lawyer . . .and the shortest and the best, if not the only way of mastering the doctrine effectually is by studying the cases in which it is embodied . . . ." Quoted in Robert Stevens, *Law School: Legal Education in America from the 1850s to the 1980s* (Chapel Hill: University of North Carolina Press, 1983), 52.

2. Vol. 1 *Pennsylvania Bar Association Reports* 118 (1895).

3. *The Pennsylvania Academy and its Women, 1850 to 1920* (Philadelphia: Pennsylvania Academy of the Fine Arts, 1973), 36–37.

Colorplate 44. Oil on canvas. Framed, 42 × 30" (106.7 × 76.2 cm). Collection of the Honorable Morris S. Arnold.

1964

Thomas Hart Benton

Thomas Hart Benton (1889–1975), American painter and muralist, was the controversial son of an equally controversial political family. A realist whose work often reflected the populist tradition of his political forebears, Benton was associated with John Steuart Curry and Grant Wood during the 1930s, when he was at the height of his fame. They were called American "regionalists," a term borrowed from a group of southern writers with strong regional interests. Benton's uninhibited self-promotion and pugnacity kept him in the public eye until his death, and he was frequently attacked by both the right and the left. In the last decades of his life, the trend toward abstract expressionism pushed his work outside the mainstream of critical attention.

Born in Missouri into a frontier family long active in politics, Benton's great-uncle, United States Senator Thomas Hart Benton had once fought with President Andrew Jackson in a street brawl. His father, Maecenas Benton, was a populist member of Congress who had expected his son to enter law and then politics. Instead, Tom chose a career in art and, after heated parental opposition, left home to work as a newspaper cartoonist. He then studied art, first in Chicago and later in Paris, returning to the United States in 1911. Until the mid-1920s Benton experimented with abstract art in New York, but then returned to Missouri and developed a more realistic focus. During subsequent travels through the country, he sketched rural Americans in their daily activities. These led to a series of murals combining historical themes and populist images with brilliant color and stylized figures.

Benton's oil painting, *Trial by Jury* (1964) reflects his long interest in law and his friendship with Lyman Field, a lawyer in Kansas City, Missouri. The painting stemmed from Benton's experience watching Field defend a damage suit in the Jackson County Circuit Court in Independence, Missouri. Field himself is shown addressing the jury in the center of the picture. Although the people have a cartoon-like quality, Benton gave careful attention to small details—like the yellow legal pad on the table. He had spent much time in courtrooms at various times in his life and considered himself quite knowledgeable in law and politics. Benton's father, before being elected to the United States Congress, had been U.S. Attorney for the Western District of Missouri. Benton himself had started a book about lawyers which he planned to illustrate, but never finished it.

Unlike most graphic portrayals of courtroom scenes which focus on the high drama of *criminal* proceedings, Benton's *Trial by Jury* shows the calmer atmosphere of a civil suit for damages. The opposing parties are seated on either side of the central table. The jury and the judge seem to be following the lawyer's argument attentively. The picture has the documentary quality of a genre painting. It lacks the humor and satire that make the work of Daumier and Rowlandson so interesting, and fails to depict the tensions felt in the earlier trial paintings by Matteson and Mulvaney. Although the parties here do not arouse our passions, Benton does convey the studied, almost clinical, atmosphere of this proceeding.

Colorplate 45. Oil on canvas. 30×40" (76×101.7 cm). The Nelson-Atkins Museum of Art, Kansas City, Missouri. Bequest of the artist.

THE PASSION OF SACCO AND VANZETTI

1931–1932

Ben Shahn

Ben Shahn (1898–1969), painter and print-maker, came to America in 1906 from Kovno, Lithuania, at the age of eight. Nicola Sacco (1891–1927) and Bartolomeo Vanzetti (1888–1927), later to become fellow-anarchists, emigrated separately from Italy in 1908. Although Shahn never met Sacco or Vanzetti, his life and art were greatly influenced by their execution for murder in 1927.

Saco and Vanzetti were arrested and tried for the murder of a paymaster and guard during a robbery at a Massachusetts shoe company in 1920. Following their conviction and death sentence, protests focused on the lack of convincing evidence against them, the prejudicial actions of the trial judge, and many procedural irregularities. As the case slowly proceeded through unsuccessful appeals and efforts to secure a pardon, the protests spread and demonstrations were held in large cities throughout the world.

By the time of their execution, on August 23, 1927, Sacco and Vanzetti had become martyrs not only to the left and the labor movement, but to a large segment of the general public. Their cause attracted the attention and support of scholars, writers, and artists. The humility and apparent honesty of the two defendants strengthened their popular appeal. Vanzetti's last speech to the court after his sentencing reflected this image:

> "If it had not been for these thing, I might have live out my life talking at street corners to scorning men. I might have die, unmarked, unknown, a failure. Now we are not a failure. This is our career and our triumph. Never in our full life could we hope to do for tolerance, for *joostice*, for man's understanding of man as now we do by accident. Our words—our lives—our pains—nothing! The taking of our lives—lives of a good shoemaker and a poor fish-peddler—all! That moment belongs to us—that agony is our triumph."[1]

Shahn, a trained lithographer and painter who had studied at the National Academy of Design and the Art Students League, was moved by the fervent demonstrations in support of Sacco and Vanzetti.

In seven months, beginning in 1930, he completed twenty-three *gouache* paintings on various aspects of the Sacco and Vanzetti case. For a mural competition at the old Museum of Modern Art, in New York, he submitted a large montage, *The Passion of Sacco and Vanzetti*, consisting of three images relating to the Sacco-Vanzetti case: a protest demonstration; a full-length portrait of the two anarchists; and a representation of the three members of the Lowell Committee standing over two coffins containing the bodies of Sacco and Vanzetti. Shahn also painted separately, in tempera, the Lowell Committee segment of the mural. This version is shown here.

The Lowell Committee, under President A. Lawrence Lowell of Harvard University, was appointed by Massachusetts Governor Fuller, to review the case and advise him. Both the committee and the governor found against the defendants, who were then executed in the electric chair. Shahn's painting, shows the committee members, sanctimoniously overlooking the coffins of Sacco and Vanzetti, with an image of the trial judge, Webster Thayer, in the background on the facade of the courthouse.

More than any other single work, this painting established Shahn as a major American artist. The case represented a continuing influence on Shahn's development as an artist deeply committed to justice and social criticism.

In August 1977, on the fiftieth anniversary of the execution, Governor Michael Dukakis of Massachusetts issued a proclamation calling the 1921 murder trial unfair because of prejudice against foreigneers and a national climate of political intolerance at the time.

1. Marion Denman Frankfurter and Gardner Jackson, eds., *The Letters of Sacco and Vanzetti* (New York: The Viking Press, 1928), [v].

Colorplate 46. Tempera on canvas. 84½ × 48" (214.6 × 121.9 cm). Whitney Museum of American Art, New York. Gift of Mr. and Mrs. Milton Lowenthal in memory of Juliana Force.

1963

Andy Warhol

Andy Warhol (1928–1987), artist, illustrator, and filmmaker, was one of the founders and main exponents of "Pop Art," the controversial *avant-garde* movement on the American art scene in the 1960s. The son of Czechoslovak working class immigrants, Warhol grew up during the depression in Pittsburgh. Having studied painting and design at the Carnegie Institute of Technology, he worked as a magazine illustrator and shoe designer. His varied experience in the highly competitive world of advertising and commercial art influenced his artistic techniques, interests, and persona.

In 1962, Warhol began to use silkscreening, a simple and inexpensive method of printing that could reproduce photographic images. He saw both the mass-production of art and the serial repetition of a single image as means of exposing the banality of America's commercial culture. Warhol was a master of self-promotion and used both the news media and his own filmmaking to promote himself, his work, and his friends. Also to convey a sense of the artist as an impersonal, shallow, and often boring celebrity. Although many considered him a charlatan and his work a profitable sham, he was taken seriously by much of the art world, and enjoyed considerable commercial success.

In 1962 and 1963 America saw a number of deaths and violent happenings which may have stimulated Andy Warhol's series of images called *Death and Disaster*.[1] The death of Marilyn Monroe in August 1962; the violent suppression of civil rights demonstrations in Birmingham, Alabama, in May 1963; and the assassination of President Kennedy in November 1963, all appear as subjects in Warhol's work. And, in his own life, Warhol's father, a West Virginia coal miner, died from drinking poisoned water when Andy was fourteen, and the atomic bomb was dropped on Hiroshima on Warhol's seventeenth birthday.

Much of Warhol's work in this period offered trenchant social commentary by its content, as much as by its technique. The *Death and Disaster* series included many images of a lone, empty

electric chair, with a "Silence" sign above and to the side of it. The chair sometimes appeared as a single image and sometimes was repeated serially in multiple images. Both versions were silkscreened on monochromatic fields of bright, vibrant colors. *Red Disaster* (1963), shown here, is, by virtue of its bright red color, one of the most shocking of the series. There were also versions in blue, lavender, orange, and silver; and some were also issued with a plain monochromatic panel in the same color added to the right.

When asked by journalists about social criticism in his work, Warhol denied that it had such meaning. His friends and many critics, however, found much of his work quite political. Although the political nature of the electric chair images is widely accepted, there are very different views of its meaning.

On August 15, 1963, the electric chair was used for the last time in New York State—at Sing Sing Prison. The actual location of the electric chair used in the *Disaster* prints is unclear, but that execution may have inspired this image.

In 1965, capital punishment was abolished in New York and remains so, despite repeated legislative efforts to reinstate it. In recent years, however, many other state legislatures have revised their capital punishment statutes to meet judicial objections to the death penalty. As a result, executions have become almost routine in a number of states.

Whether it was intended as a political statement, *Red Disaster* and Warhol's other electric chair images have conveyed to many the horror of capital punishment. In that regard, at least, it continues a long tradition of art exposing inhumanity in the administration of criminal law.

1. *Andy Warhol: Death and Disaster* (Houston: The Menil Foundation and the Houston Fine Arts Press, 1988).

Colorplate 47. Silkscreen on linen. 93×80¼" (236.2×203.8 cm). Museum of Fine Arts, Boston. Charles H. Bayley Picture and Painting Fund. Copyright 1990 The Estate and Foundation of Andy Warhol ARS, New York.

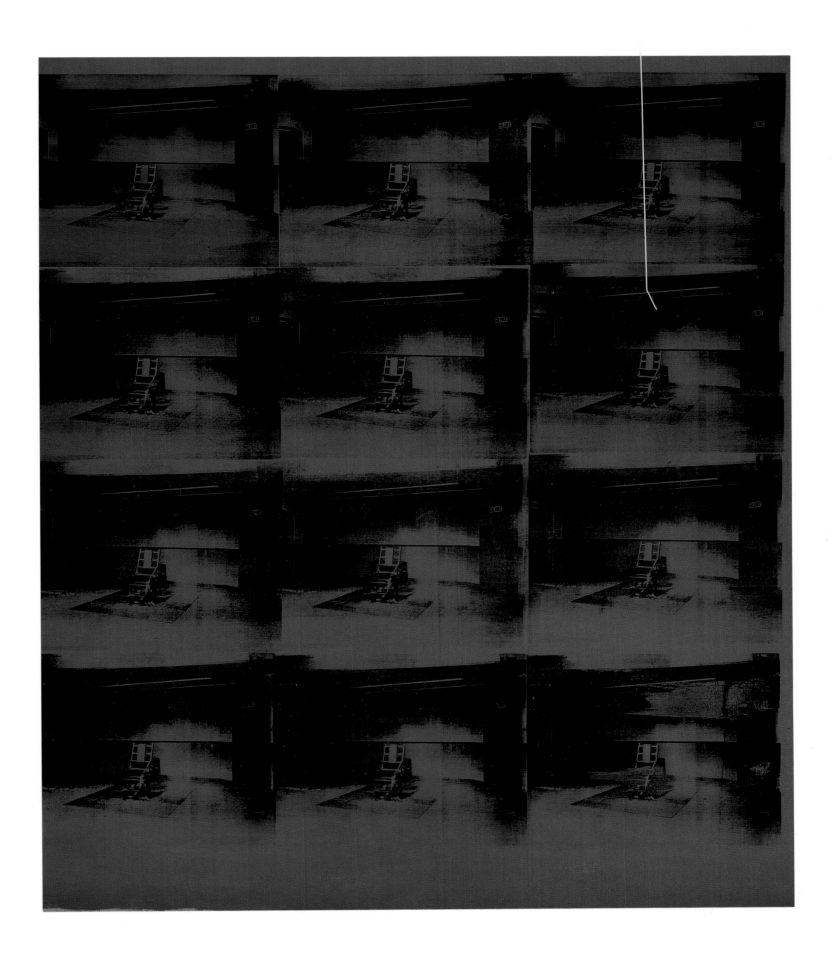

1963

Norman Rockwell

For over fifty years, Norman Rockwell's magazine covers and illustrations made him the most popular artist in America. Rockwell (1894–1978), using carefully crafted detail, homespun humor, and sentimentality, created 322 covers for the *Saturday Evening Post* from 1916 to 1963. His work, glorifying traditional and usually conservative American values, was loved by the public, but dismissed by the art world as slick, superficial, inauthentic, and lacking artistic merit.

In the early 1960s Rockwell's work underwent a partial but significant change. In 1963, he ended his long association with the conservative *Saturday Evening Post*, and began a relationship with the more socially conscious *Look* magazine. With *Look*, the subject matter of Rockwell's paintings broadened to include some of the momentous issues that were shaking American society at the time. These included, for example, *The Problem We All Live With* (shown here), which appeared in *Look* on January 14, 1964; *Southern Justice: Murder in Mississippi* (*Look*, June 29, 1965); *How Goes the War on Poverty?* (*Look*, July 27, 1965); and *Blood Brothers*, a poster done for the Congress of Racial Equality (CORE) in the late 60s. Some of these, particularly *Southern Justice* and *Blood Brothers*, employed a more impressionistic and compelling technique which had not been seen in Rockwell's previous work, and which he would not often use again.

Perhaps some of the same violent events that had influenced Andy Warhol in the turbulent years of 1963 and 1964 had a similar, but less horrific effect on Rockwell. The brutal reaction to the civil rights movement seemed to affect him most. School desegregation, in the face of active resistance throughout the south, was stalled in many states. The bombing of the Sixteenth Street Church in Birmingham, Alabama, in September 1963, killing four schoolgirls, shocked the country. Terrorism, angry mobs, and racist police officials were shown regularly on television suppressing desegregation efforts.

In the January 14, 1964, issue of *Look* magazine, Rockwell's painting with the unwieldy title,

The Problem We All Live With, appeared without accompanying text or explanation. The issue was in fact largely devoted to housing problems. The picture portrayed a young black girl (modeled on a child in Rockwell's neighborhood in Stockbridge, Massachusetts), being escorted into school by four large United States marshals, two in front and two behind her. By cropping the bodies of the marshals, attention is focused on the small figure of the girl, heightening our sense of her strength, dignity, and vulnerability. The wide space in the center of the picture between the girl and the two rear marshals (a boldly asymmetrical composition for Rockwell) showed the red remains of a ripe tomato which had just missed its target. That could be seen as the artist's watered-down reference to the Birmingham bomb explosion, or simply his rendition of a not uncommon scene in many southern towns and cities. The painting aroused considerable sympathy for the courageous black children who had borne the brunt of the attacks on desegregation since the landmark Supreme Court decision in the case of *Brown vs. Board of Education of Topeka* (1954).

Later that year, Congress passed the Civil Rights Act of 1964, which, among other things, required all school districts to comply with its provisions against segregation, or lose federal funds. Progress continued, but ever so slowly. America then discovered that segregated schools were not a solely southern issue, and that the struggle in northern cities was no less painful or complex. Today, of course, *The Problem We all Live With*, remains very much with us, although it no longer seems as simple an issue as Rockwell presented in 1964.

1. L.N. Moffatt, *Norman Rockwell, a Definitive Catalogue* (Stockbridge, Mass.: The Norman Rockwell Museum at Stockbridge, 1986), 2:692.

Colorplate 48. Oil on canvas. 36 × 58″ (91.4 × 147.3 cm). The Norman Rockwell Museum at Stockbridge, Massachusetts. Printed by permission of the Estate of Norman Rockwell. Copyright (©) 1964 Estate of Norman Rockwell.